CHRISTIAN ETHICS FOR MODERN MAN

DECISIONS! DECISIONS!

George A. Chauncey

CARTOONS BY JIM CRANE

 JOHN KNOX PRESS
Richmond, Virginia

Scripture quotations are from the *Revised Standard Version of the Bible,* copyrighted 1946 and 1952.

Library of Congress Cataloging in Publication Data

Chauncey, George A   1927-
   Decisions! Decisions!
   (Christian ethics for modern man)   (Chime paperbacks)
   Bibliography: p.
   1. Christian ethics.   I.   Title.
BJ1251.C476   241   73-161841
ISBN 0-8042-9090-3

© John Knox Press 1972
Printed in the United States of America

General Editor's Foreword

Christian Ethics for Modern Man is a series of brief and easy-to-read books on moral issues in contemporary social problems. The books do not provide or pretend to provide the Christian with answers to the complex problems confronting modern man. They do offer guidance to Christians searching for their own answers. The purpose of the series is to help persons make moral judgments more responsibly.

Decisions! Decisions! by George A. Chauncey analyzes the elements that go into any moral judgment and suggests ways one's faith in God can, ought to, and sometimes does influence his moral decisions.

Rich Man Poor Man by Donald W. Shriver, Jr., discusses some of the moral issues American Christians face as they participate in and benefit from the American economy. The book incorporates and comments on recorded conversations among Christian theologians, businessmen, labor leaders, and consumers on those moral issues.

Foreign Policy Is Your Business by Theodore R. Weber examines some of the moral issues faced by a government and its citizens in the development and conduct of foreign policy. Examples: Under what conditions ought a nation go to war? How should the U.S.A. relate to Communist governments? Is it ever right for a government to deceive its own citizens?

These books have been written not only for individual study but also for group discussion. *Leader's Guide to Christian Ethics for Modern Man* by Richard F. Perkins offers valuable suggestions for the use of these books by groups.

George A. Chauncey
GENERAL EDITOR

CONTENTS

INTRODUCTION

"Johnny should not have hit his little sister quite that hard."

"Our principal is hopelessly square."

"The United States has an obligation to help free nations defend themselves against Communist aggression."

"That's a no-no."

"The welfare system is a national disgrace."

"You're a good man, Charlie Brown."

These are moral judgments—that is, judgments about what is morally right or wrong, good or bad, required or forbidden. This book concerns such judgments. It assumes that everybody makes them; that most people, most of the time, want to make them as responsibly as possible; and that people can grow in their ability to make moral judgments responsibly by reflecting on the judgments which they and others actually make. This book offers help for such reflection.

Chapter 1 opens with a dramatic sketch in which people express a variety of moral judgments. These judgments are examined to see what they have in common. It is concluded that every moral judgment involves four components: some expression of the *person* making the judgment, his *perception* or interpretation of what he is judging, his *principles* or standard for measuring right or wrong, and his *procedure* or method for relating principles and perceptions.

Chapter 2 clarifies these components. Chapter 3 discusses the role which a person's religious faith or basic commitment in life plays in his moral judgment-making. Chapter 4 lists factors influencing one's perception of what he judges. Chapters 5, 6, and 7 deal with moral principles or standards. Chapter 8 proposes a procedure for responsible judgment-making.

This book might be subtitled "The Moral Judgments of a Christian." In each section I try to indicate, first, some ways in which the judgments of Christians are like those of other people, and then, secondly, some differences which faith in the God and Father of Jesus Christ can, ought to, and sometimes does make in the moral judgments of Christians.

Two American theologians have influenced my thinking about Christian ethics more than any others: the late H. Richard Niebuhr, under whom I took a course in Christian ethics at Yale Divinity School twenty years ago, and James M. Gustafson, Niebuhr's successor, under whom I have never studied, but from whom I have learned much. My indebtedness to both men will be apparent to all persons familiar with their writings. Neither man, of course, is responsible for what follows.

GEORGE A. CHAUNCEY

1 | What Is a Moral Judgment?

Just as the teacher clears his throat to call the adult church school class to order, Mrs. Jones dashes into the room.

MRS. JONES: I was never so embarrassed in my life. Did you see it?

MR. BROWN: See what? —

MRS. JONES: Reverend Long's picture on the front page of the morning papers. Demonstrating! With a bunch of welfare mothers at the welfare office!

MRS. SMITH: Oh, no! How awful!

MR. BROWN: I didn't see it. I haven't looked at the morning paper yet. What happened?

MRS. JONES: What happened was that Tom Long—the Reverend Thomas J. Long, *our* minister—went with a group of welfare mothers down to the welfare office and *demanded* an increase in welfare payments. I think it's just disgraceful. Why a so-called man of God would do something like that simply baffles me. Already this morning three of my friends in the garden club have called to ask me why he did it. I told them I didn't know why he did it, but that *I* certainly didn't approve his action.

MR. WILSON: Why do you feel it was wrong?

MRS. JONES: Well, for one thing, I don't believe in demonstrating. I am all for citizens' taking an active role in civic affairs, and I've done a lot of telephoning and letter-writing and visiting Council members on behalf of the garden club. But I don't believe in marching in the streets. And particularly not for more welfare. Goodness, we give those people enough of our hard-earned tax money now. When are they ever going to be satisfied? All some of those women do is produce more babies so they'll get more money. I call it subsidized immorality, and . . .

MRS. SMITH: Yes. And you can't get any of them to work these days. I've been trying for months to find some woman to come clean for me just one day a week, but most of them are simply too lazy to earn a living.

MR. BLAKE: What concerns me is not the welfare issue, or even that the welfare mothers demonstrated. What bothers me is that Tom Long demonstrated with those women. I'm church treasurer this year, and last night, after Tom's marching was shown on TV, four members of this church called me and canceled their pledges. They said they weren't going to support a church whose preacher marched for larger welfare checks. I dread to think how many more calls I'll get.

MR. WILSON: Yeah, Jim, I know we'll lose some pledges because Tom marched, and we may even lose a few members. But Tom can't let his every action be determined by the feelings of the more conservative members of our congregation, can he? I personally wish Tom hadn't marched, but I've got to admire his integrity. He feels strongly that welfare allocations are inadequate, and that the government has an obligation to provide more funds.

MR. BLAKE: Yes, but why did he *march?*

MR. WILSON: Well, as you know, Jim, Tom has been

working for some time with the local group of welfare mothers. They decided last Monday they'd
march on the welfare office and asked Tom to march
with them. He knew he'd get a lot of flak if he did
it, but he thought it was the right thing for him
to do, so he told them he would march. I heard
about the plans and called Tom, urging him not
to do it because I knew it would split this church
wide open. But Tom said he had promised to march,
so he was going to march. I believe that a man
ought to keep his promises, and I'm confident that
Tom sincerely thought he was doing the right thing.

MRS. SMITH: I don't doubt his sincerity. I doubt his
common sense. I think it was wrong for him to do
something that he knew would offend so many of
us.

MRS. MILLER: Well, I—for one—am glad that he
marched! I think a minister ought to be concerned
with social problems and ought to get involved—
even if that means marching in the streets. It's precisely because he does things like that that my son—
and lots of other young people—still come to this
church. I personally loved Reverend Short, but you
know that no young people ever *voluntarily* came
to church while he was here.

MRS. JONES: My dear, I think we're all interested in
young people (they are the future of the church,
you know), and we're all for applying the principles
of Christianity to everyday life. What we're talking
about now, however, isn't young people or everyday
Christianity. What we're talking about now is that
the minister of this church, whose salary we pay,
participated yesterday in a demonstration at the
welfare office. He was on TV last night, and had

his picture on the front page of this morning's paper. I personally think that my minister did wrong and that I have a duty to protest his action. Furthermore . . .

TEACHER: I hate to interrupt this lively discussion, but I think we'd better get to our lesson. We're still studying the Sermon on the Mount, and our text for his morning is Matthew 7:1-5. Would you please read it for us, Mrs. Smith?

MRS. SMITH: Certainly. Let me find it. Oh, here it is: "Judge not, that you be not judged. . . ."

Despite the warning of Jesus, all of us do it.

We judge others. And ourselves. And actions and agents. Character and conduct. Motives and intentions. Causes and consequences. Ends and means. Preachers, politicians, policemen, policies, pronouncements, procedures.

We praise some things and call them right or good.

We condemn other things and call them wrong or evil.

And in this regard—at least—we follow the example of one who praised the generosity of a poor widow, condemned the hypocrisy of religious leaders, and offered a good many guidelines for the good life in addition to his strange warning about not judging others.

This book concerns moral judgments. In this chapter I want to explain what I mean by a moral judgment and to invite you to analyze the moral judgments expressed in our dramatic sketch.

Here's my definition: A moral judgment is an evaluation of a person (or group) or his (its) behavior in light of some standard.

1. A moral judgment is an *evaluation*—that is, a feeling, belief, attitude, or conviction about the value of something. In moral judgments we declare that things are right or wrong, good or bad, better or worse, responsible or irresponsible, required or forbidden. When you say that something is desirable, you are making a moral judgment. When you praise or blame someone for something, you are making a moral judgment. When you decide that something is your duty, you are making a moral judgment. When you conclude that your church or your government ought or ought not to do something, you are making a moral judgment. Here are some of the moral judgments made or suggested in our dramatic sketch:

Oh, no! How awful!

What Rev. Long did was wrong.

What Rev. Long did was right.

Demonstrations are wrong.

Demonstrations are right, or at least morally permissible.

Some welfare mothers produce more babies so they will get more money, and that is wrong.

No welfare mothers are willing to work these days, and everyone ought to be willing to work.

A man ought to keep his promises.

One ought not to do things which he knows will offend lots of people.

Rev. Long is a man of integrity, and that is good.

Rev. Long was sincere, and sincerity is praiseworthy.

Rev. Long didn't show common sense, and that is reprehensible.

A minister ought to be concerned with social problems.

A minister has particular obligations to those who
pay his salary.

2. What we evaluate in moral judgments are *persons*
or their *behavior*. We sometimes use evaluative language
in referring to or addressing nonhumans, such as pets.
Thus a man might say of his dog, "He's a good dog,"
and mean that the dog not only hunts birds well but is
loyal, trustworthy, obedient, kind, reverent, and the like.

Or, if the man's dog is like mine, not completely house-broken (my dog is an obedience school dropout!), the man might often look the dog right in the face, shake his finger at him, and say in a stern, firm voice, "Bad dog! Bad dog!" But while we use *evaluative* language about pets and other things, our moral judgments are about people—their motives, intentions, character, and the like —and their actions.

One can distinguish two basic types of moral judgments: judgments of moral rightness or wrongness, on the one hand, and judgments of moral worth, on the other. It is helpful to keep this distinction in mind. The things talked about in the two types of judgments are different. Judgments of moral rightness or wrongness deal with specific acts: Was it right or wrong for Mr. Long to march? Did he perform his duty or violate it by participating in the demonstration? Judgments of moral worth, on the other hand, deal not with particular acts, but with persons, motives, intentions, traits of character, and the like: What sort of man is Long? Is he a man of integrity? What was his intention in marching? Was he sincere?

This distinction between an action, on the one hand, and the motive that prompted it or the person who did it, on the other, comes in very handy when we evaluate good deeds done from shady motives or stupid things done with the best of intentions, or when we are tempted to condemn rather harshly a person or group on the basis of one particular action that offends us.

I have said that we evaluate persons or their actions. It would be more precise to say that we evaluate persons or their actions *as we perceive them,* because what we judge is not so much the person himself as our perception of him, not so much the action itself as our interpretation of the action. For example, what did Mr. Long do? The different ways the people in our sketch answered that apparently "factual" question greatly influenced their different judgments of his behavior.

3. Moral judgments are evaluations made in light of some *standard* or rule or criterion. All of us carry around with us a bagful of moral rules, laws, principles, values, guidelines, or norms of some sort which we use in making our moral judgments. An act is right or wrong depending on whether it does or does not measure up to our moral standard. I do not mean to imply by this that moral judgment-making is a completely rational process. Far from it! Not all of our rules, principles, values, or guidelines are articulated or even in our consciousness; the moral principles we are conscious of often conflict with one another; and we do not normally reach our moral conclusions by cool, dispassionate, deductive reasoning, moving from moral principle to factual premise to logical conclusion. In our dramatic presentation, for example, Mrs. Jones seemed somewhat emotionally involved in her judgment about her minister's marching! However, all of us have some sort of moral standard.

A moral standard can be simply one's feelings. Ernest Hemingway's standard was, "What's good is what I feel good after, and what's bad is what I feel bad after." [1] Normally, however, when pressed to justify a particular judgment, one cites not just a moral feeling ("I just felt that it was wrong"), but also or instead a moral rule ("A man ought not to beat his wife"). And when pressed to defend a moral rule, one usually cites a more general moral principle. For example, one might argue like this: Mr. Long should not have demonstrated.

Why? What made his action wrong? He should not have demonstrated because demonstrations are wrong. Why? What makes demonstrations wrong? Demonstrations are wrong because they disturb the peace, inconvenience traffic, split congregations, and encourage riots. In a word, they produce bad consequences, and acts which result in bad consequences are wrong.

Different people, communities, and cultures, of course, have different moral standards or codes of conduct. What one group calls right, another may label wrong. Moreover, it often appears that the same person plays the moral game by one set of rules in one situation and another set in another. Furthermore, as we have commented, often we are not entirely conscious of the standard by which we judge things to be right or wrong, and occasionally, when the standard by which we are measuring behavior is pointed out to us, we are not particularly proud of it. But consciously or unconsciously, wisely or foolishly, rightly or wrongly, we measure actions and motives, individuals and groups, ourselves and others by some standard.

4. Moral judgments are made by some *procedure,* that is, through some method. I decide what I ought to do in a given situation by some means or other. I may conclude that it is my duty to do so-and-so by carefully weighing the options before me. I may deliberate on some general moral principle and deduce that such-and-such an act would be wrong. I may ask my pastor, mother, scoutmaster, fraternity brother, or boss what I ought to do. I may simply "sense" or "intuit" my responsibility. I may let "love" reveal to me my obligations. I may depend on the Holy Spirit to guide me. But by some process I arrive at my judgment. The debate on

"situation ethics" or the "new morality" is a debate over—among other things—the proper procedure to use in making moral judgments.

5. Finally, moral judgments are made by *people*— that is, by men and women of flesh and blood who bring to their judgment-making situations not only standards and procedures, but also dispositions, attitudes, desires, frustrations, interests, prejudices, imaginations, sensitivities, experiences, and a whole host of other personal and social factors that go into making them the persons they are. In every moral judgment there is some expression of the judge's character, commitments, and concerns.

In sum, a moral judgment is a person's evaluation of human conduct or character as he perceives it, in light of some standard or principle, through some process. My compulsion for alliteration makes me identify the four key components in a moral judgment as these:

the *person* making the judgment,

his *perception* of what he judges,

his *principles* or standard, and

his *procedure* for judgment-making.

We will look at each of these four components in the chapters that follow. Meanwhile, I invite you to analyze the judgments made about Mr. Long's action by the characters in our opening dramatic sketch and to compare their judgments with your own.

QUESTIONS FOR THOUGHT AND DISCUSSION
1. Find and list the moral judgments about Long's action made by Mrs. Jones, Mrs. Miller, Mr. Blake, and Mr. Wilson.

2. Analyze these judgments by considering three questions:

a. How did each of the four *perceive* Long's action?

b. By what *principles* did they judge his action to be right or wrong?

c. What do their judgments tell you about them as *persons?*

3. What is your own judgment about Long's act? On what grounds have you made your judgment?

4. Compare your judgment with that of the persons in the sketch with whom you disagree. How do you answer their arguments? How do you think they would answer yours? What does your evaluation of their judgments reveal about your own perceptions, principles, and personal commitments, loyalties, and interests?

5. Evaluate your evaluations of their evaluations in light of the Bible. You may find that this is not as easy to do as it first appears. People can find support for a variety of positions in Holy Writ.

a. If you tend to approve of Long's action, for example, you can look up the word "welfare" in a concordance and come up with these biblical gems supporting your point of view: Nehemiah 2:10; Esther 10:3; Philippians 2:19-21. Or you can argue that Jesus led the first Christian demonstration, citing Matthew 21:1-11.

b. If you tend to disapprove of Long's action, you can find all sorts of biblical condemnations for pastors who upset the flock, such as Jeremiah 23:1-4 or Ezekiel 34:1-10, or you can cite an interesting first-century moral rule saying that those who don't work shouldn't be allowed to eat, 2 Thessalonians 3:10.

c. If you don't want to play games with Scripture, you might evaluate Long's action in light of these two passages: 1 Corinthians 8:1-13, especially verse 9, and 10:23-30, especially verse 29b.

d. If you don't know how in the world to relate the Bible to contemporary moral dilemmas, you might wrestle for a while with this question: How in the world does one relate the Bible to contemporary moral dilemmas?

2 | How to Analyze Moral Judgments

Everybody makes moral judgments, and no matter whose it is—the Pope's, the President's, your pastor's, or yours—every moral judgment involves four components: some expression of the *person* making the judgment; his *perception* or interpretation of what he is judging; his *principles* or standard for measuring right or wrong; and his *procedure* or methodology for relating principles and perceptions. You can analyze any moral judgment you run into by examining these four features.

At the end of the last chapter I suggested that you look at the dramatic presentation which opened that chapter, and with the first three of these components in mind, analyze the judgments made by Mrs. Jones, Mr. Blake, Mrs. Miller, and Mr. Wilson. In this chapter I will follow that suggestion myself and make a few observations about what turns up.

Mrs. Jones and Mr. Blake disapproved of Long's action. Mrs. Miller and Mr. Wilson—with different degrees of enthusiasm—thought their pastor did the right thing. We want to discover why. We'll begin with their perceptions.

Perceptions

Mrs. Jones' perception of what Long did was something like this: He demonstrated. He demonstrated for increased welfare payments. He appeared on the TV news last night. He got his picture on the front page of the morning paper. He embarrassed her. He baffled her. He prompted three of her garden club friends to ask her why in the world her pastor was marching in the streets.

Mr. Blake's version of what happened: Long demonstrated with some welfare mothers. He received lots of publicity doing it. He made a lot of people in the church mad. He prompted four members to cancel their pledges. He made Blake's job a lot harder, because Blake is church treasurer.

Mr. Wilson's assessment of the case: Long marched. He decided to do so after careful reflection. It seemed to him to be his duty. His marching was consistent with his conviction that welfare payments were too low and with his relationship with a group of welfare mothers. In marching he fulfilled a promise.

Mrs. Miller's statement of "the facts": Long marched because of his concern for social problems and his willingness to practice what he preached. By marching he evoked new admiration from her son and other young people, and thereby increased their interest in the church.

This summary of the ways in which the different persons "saw" what Long did prompts four observations:

1. What we evaluate in our moral judgments is always *interpreted* action, never merely the action itself. No one cared one way or the other about the physiological reality of Long's walking—that is, of his placing one foot in front of the other and thereby moving down the street. Long didn't just go for a walk. He marched. He demonstrated. He split the congregation. He kept a promise. He influenced young people.

2. Our moral judgments depend—in part—on how we interpret actions. We call them as we see them. If we see them in one way, we call them right. If we see

them in another, we call them wrong. Blake evaluated an action which, for him, was primarily a church-splitting action. Wilson, in contrast, judged a promise-keeping action. If Wilson had been more impressed by the church-splitting character of Long's action or if Blake had been more impressed by its promise-keeping nature, their judgments might well have been different. Differences in perception are a principal cause of disagreement in judgment. They are not the sole cause by any means, but they are a common one.

3. All of us hold that moral judgments should be based on "the facts of the case." Moreover, all of us believe that our moral judgments *are* based on the facts of the case, and we tend to feel that all reasonable people who know the real facts (and have sensible moral standards) will agree with us in our judgments. That's why a large part of moral argumentation consists of attempts to persuade others to face "reality," to recognize "the truth" about the situation—which usually means, to agree with *our* reading of what the situation is. Wilson said, in effect, to Blake: "Sure, so a few hotheads got mad. The main thing to realize about what Long did is that he kept a promise."

4. All descriptions of situations are themselves forms of evaluation. We do not look at all the facts and then make our judgment; the very selection of *which* facts to look at is itself a judgment. No one mentioned, for example, what color shirt Long wore, or whether he smoked his pipe as he walked down the street, or where he was in the line. All these points—and thousands more —are "facts" about what Long did. They were not mentioned because they seemed unimportant. But decisions about what is important and what is unimportant in

assessing a situation are preliminary forms of moral judgment and greatly influence our final judgment about the rightness or wrongness of an action.

So much for now about perceptions. In chapter 4 we'll consider some factors which influence what we see as we look at actions and situations. Let's turn now to the standard by which our friends praised or condemned their pastor's act.

Principles

Every moral judgment is made in light of some moral standard or criterion or set of principles. An act is right if it measures up to this standard, wrong if it does not.

A typical moral standard is a very loosely organized collection of only partially articulated moral values, convictions, commitments, and feelings. It usually contains some rather specific *moral rules* (e.g., help old ladies cross the street—if, that is, they want to cross the street) and some rather general *moral principles* (e.g., be kind to others). It is undergirded by an *ethical theory*—often unrecognized—about what makes an act right or wrong (e.g., an act is right if and only if it expresses love). Moreover, every standard assumes some great *source of value* (e.g., pleasure, one's nation, humanity, God) which one embraces in faith and accepts as the underlying basis for his standard.

Ordinarily one ought to be able to justify his rules by his principles, and his principles by his ethical theory. Thus: Why should one help old ladies cross the street? Because one should be kind to others. Why should one be kind? Because one ought to love others, and kindness is an expression of love. In moral arguments we ask our opponents to justify their judgments like this, as we shall see in a moment. However, I don't want to give the impression that in practice moral standards are nice, neatly organized sets of clearly articulated rules, principles, theories, and beliefs, each of which has been reasonably inferred from the more basic moral conviction above it— because they are not! Our moral rules come from a variety of sources, not simply by inference from our principles; they are not always consistent with each other; and often we are not even aware—until we are challenged—of what rules we use in making our judgments.

However, we do ordinarily use rules in making judgments. We also use them in justifying those judgments to others. Sometimes when we justify our judgments to others, we make our moral rules quite explicit. At other times, we assume that any old fool ought to know what moral rules or principles we are basing our judgment on. Examples:

Mrs. Jones thought that Long ought not to have demonstrated. Why? Because she didn't "believe in" demonstrations—that is, she regarded demonstrations as wrong in themselves. Moreover, she regarded the cause for which Long demonstrated—increased welfare payments—as a bad or evil cause. The rules by which she justified her judgment were these: One ought not to do things which are wrong in themselves, and one ought not to support evil causes.

Mr. Blake criticized Long's action on the grounds that it prompted four members of the congregation to cancel their pledges. His (implicit) justifying rule: Ministers ought not to do things that will provoke economic boycotts of the church.

Mrs. Miller supported her pastor's action in light of two moral rules: A minister ought to work for social justice, and a minister ought to try to keep young people interested in church.

Mr. Wilson reluctantly accepted what his pastor did on the basis of these rules: A man ought to do what he feels it is his duty to do, and a man ought to keep his promises.

What can we say about rules, principles, and standards in light of these examples? Four observations:

1. One reason we differ in our moral judgments is that we use different moral rules in making these judgments. Because this is the case, one thing we try to do in moral arguments is to demonstrate the superiority of our rules to those of the person with whom we differ. We usually do this by (a) declaring that the rule which the other fellow cites is not really a valid or binding rule, or (b) arguing that our moral rule is more binding in this particular situation than his is.

a. Wilson challenged the validity of Blake's rule. Blake implied that ministers ought not to do things that provoke economic boycotts. In response to this, Wilson said, "Tom can't let his every action be determined by the feelings of the more conservative members of our congregation, can he?" In challenging the validity of Blake's (implicit) rule, Wilson was calling for Blake to justify his rule. Wilson was asking: By what standard did Blake consider his rule to be a valid standard for judging ministerial behavior? Why should a minister never do anything to provoke an economic boycott? (You might ask yourself: What would count as a good reason in support of Blake's rule? What would count against it?)

You can discover your own or another's moral theory and object of faith by persistently asking: Why? On what grounds? How do you justify that? Moral rules are justified by moral principles, which in turn are justified by moral theories, which in turn are justified by one's ultimate moral (or religious) commitment—which cannot be justified but only affirmed in faith. More about that in chapter 3.

b. Sometimes, then, we challenge the validity of another's rule. More frequently, we acknowledge that rule's validity as a rule, "other things being equal," but argue that in the case at hand our rule is more binding. Mrs. Jones, for example, conceded the validity of Mrs. Miller's concern for young people and thus of her rule that ministers ought to do things that would keep young people interested in church. Other things being equal, Mrs. Jones would probably agree with Mrs. Miller that an action of Long's was right if it attracted young people, wrong if it repelled them ("they're the future of the church, you know"). But other things were not equal (they hardly ever are!), so in this particular case—the demonstration—the positive fact that Long attracted young people didn't count nearly as much for Mrs. Jones as the negative fact that it was by its nature a wrong act.

A basic ethical question—once again—is, By what standard do you justify your standard? On what grounds do you decide that Moral Rule A is more binding than Moral Rule B—particularly if you accept both of them?

2. We tend in judging an act to focus attention on a particular dimension of that act. Every moral act has at least four dimensions: the *motive* that prompts it; the *intentions* of the agent; its own *character* as an act; and the *consequences* that flow from it. Some standards deal with motives, others with intentions, others with the act's nature, and still others with consequences. We tend to judge an entire act in light of our rule or standard regarding one of its dimensions.

Some standards deal with the *character* of the act— that is, with the act itself apart from its motives, the intentions of its agent, or its consequences. We have already noted that Mrs. Jones condemned Long's act because she thought that demonstrating was a method of exercising citizenship which was wrong in itself. According to her, one ought not to demonstrate regardless of the situation; there is no possible justification for this sort of activity. Mrs. Jones probably felt the same way about lying or stealing or cheating as she did about demonstrating. She almost certainly felt the same way about rape or adultery or torture. These are all acts which are simply wrong in themselves. To do any of them is to do wrong. Many people who would not agree with Mrs. Jones about the wrong-in-itself character of demonstrating would share her judgments about rape or adultery or torture.

Other standards deal with *motive* and *intentions*. One's motive is what moves him to take an action; his intention is what he aims at in that action. Thus I can be moved by love (motive) to give my daughter pleasure (intention) by taking her to the fair. But my motive in taking her to the fair could be guilt feelings instead of love, and my intention could be to demonstrate what a fine and thoughtful father I am, not to give her joy.

Wilson focused his attention on Long's motive and intentions. He felt that Long's motive was good (he was sincere), and that his intentions were noble (he wanted to help get increased welfare payments). Long felt obligated to march. Thus, even though Wilson had severe reservations about the wisdom of his pastor's participation in the demonstration, he was willing to grant Long the right to march because Long obviously felt that it was his duty.

Blake and Mrs. Miller judged the act in light of its *consequences*. Blake considered the act wrong because it resulted in what he regarded as bad consequences: four members canceled their pledges. Mrs. Miller, on the other hand, considered it right because it resulted in what she considered to be good consequences: her son came to church that morning without fussing.

3. It seems less than wise to judge an act in light of a single dimension to the exclusion of the other three dimensions.

Mrs. Jones condemned Long for marching because she felt that marching was wrong in itself. According to her, it was Long's duty not to march because one ought not to do things that are wrong. But suppose Long had felt it his duty to march and yet had refused to do his duty because he was lazy, or scared, or wanted to watch football on TV. How would Mrs. Jones evaluate his act if she knew all that? How do you judge a "right" act done from an "evil" motive?

Wilson praised Long's motive and intentions. Long was sincere and meant well. He felt it his duty to demonstrate. If the teacher hadn't cut off the discussion to get on with the lesson, Wilson might well have said to Mrs. Jones, "Don't you believe that a man ought to do what he feels is his duty? Aren't you going to give him the moral freedom to follow the dictates of his own conscience? Don't you remember that glorious moment when the Apostles said, 'We must obey God rather than men!' or when Luther declared, 'Here I stand'?"

These are moving words, and they might well have silenced Mrs. Jones. On the other hand, Mrs. Jones might well have responded: "Are you seriously contending that motive alone makes an act right? Are you willing to grant a man the moral right to do *anything,* as long as his conscience demands that he do it? Just how far down that line are you prepared to go? You say that it is okay for our minister to demonstrate because he feels he ought

to. Would you be willing for him to engage in civil disobedience if his conscience compelled him to? How
about destroying welfare records as a sign of protest
against a dehumanizing system? How about bombing the
welfare office? Or kidnapping the welfare administrator?"
(Don't just sit there, Wilson. Speak up!)

Blake and Mrs. Miller judged the act in light of its
consequences. The norm they both used is that an act
is right if and only if it produces or is intended to produce more good than any possible alternative act could.
The fact that they used the same norm and came up
with different judgments about Long's act points up some
of the difficulties of this norm. How do you measure
consequences? What are good consequences? By what
criteria do you judge them good? For whom are they
good? Even if one could answer all those questions, he
would still be faced with the problem, Do good ends
justify any means? Assume for a moment that maintain-
ing the "peace and harmony" of the church is a good
and desirable end. Does that mean that the minister
should never do anything that would upset anyone? Or
assume that increased welfare payments is a good and
desirable goal. Is any sort of action aimed at producing
this result morally permissible?

4. Final observation about standards and principles:
Nice, neat, easy-to-apply, ever ready, and always depend-
able criteria for telling right from wrong aren't nearly as
easy to come by as one might at first suppose.

People

What we decide in making a moral judgment depends not just on what we see and what standard we
use but also—most of all—on who we are. And who we

are depends primarily on our relationships: horizontal relationships—our place and roles in society; and vertical relationships—our commitments to objects which mean most to us.

One can easily identify some of the horizontal relationships which played such a major role in making the participants in our drama the people they are. It is quite reasonable to assume that these people are all white, middle- or upper-middle-class Protestants. They demonstrate typical (stereotyped?) WASP attitudes toward welfare, welfare recipients, and demonstrations. Their understanding of the "peace of the church" is a cultural rather than a biblical one. Their expectations of the role of their pastor are drawn more from the customs of middle America than from the New Testament. Their remarks give no indication that any one of them has ever lived in a slum, suffered financial deprivation, or endured the indignities of applying for welfare.

The reasonableness of these guesses about the socio-economic character of our group can be demonstrated by surveys of public opinion—such as those reported by Jeffrey K. Hadden in his book *The Gathering Storm in the Churches*[1]—or, more simply, just by considering how different the conversation would have been if the group discussing the moral propriety of Long's action had been (1) the welfare mothers with whom he marched, (2) the members of the Friendship Class at St. James AME Zion Church, (3) university students, or even (4) the senior high sons and daughters of Mrs. Jones, Mrs. Miller, Blake, Wilson, and others, who were meeting at that very moment downstairs!

We are all influenced in our moral judgments by our time and place and companions in history. Others shape and condition who we are and what we stand for. We are social selves through and through, and we have no existence apart from our relationships with others. But who we are and what we stand for depends not just on horizontal relationships but also on vertical ones— our commitments to God or the gods. Waldo Beach once wrote, "We do as we are, and we are as we love—meaning by love: ultimate attachment." [2] We'll examine in the next chapter the significance of one's faith for his moral judgments.

QUESTIONS FOR THOUGHT AND DISCUSSION

1. How would Tom Long have described what he did? How would the welfare mothers have perceived his action?

2. Blake saw Long's act as a church-splitting one, Wilson as a promise-keeping one. If other things were equal, do you think a minister should (*a*) keep a promise even if it involves splitting a congregation, or (*b*) avoid splitting a congregation even if this involves breaking a promise? Justify your answer.

3. The author distinguishes four dimensions of a moral act: its motive, intentions, character, and consequences. Test how you weigh the different dimensions by examining your feelings about these acts:

a. Your eight-year-old son, playing "catch" in the front yard, accidentally throws a ball through the living-room window.

b. Your son accidentally breaks the window even though you told him just last week not to play catch in the front yard anymore.

c. A prisoner of war reveals military secrets after being subjected to torture.

d. A prisoner of war earns an extra food ration by informing the guards of a plan to escape.

e. A genuinely sincere "conscientious objector" refuses to cooperate at all with the selective service system.

f. A soldier shoots an old woman in a rice paddy, thinking she might be an enemy soldier, but not knowing for sure.

g. A concentration camp commander executes thousands of Jews because he has been ordered to do so.

h. The President of the United States denies that our government has U-2 planes flying over the Soviet Union, even though it has such flights. The world believes him, so he gets away with it.

i. The President denies that a U-2 plane has been spying on the Soviet Union, and the Soviet Union produces evidence that he is lying.

4. Look at some teachings of Jesus which seem to deal with motive (Matt. 5:8, 21-22, 27-28), intention (Matt. 6:1, 5, 7, 16-18), specific acts (Matt. 5:21-22, 33-42), and consequences (Matt. 7:16-20, 24-27). Where do you think Jesus put his emphasis? On what grounds do you think this?

3 | PERSONS: In Whom Do You Trust?

". . . the great ethical question is always the question of faith, 'In what does man trust?' "[1] So wrote H. Richard Niebuhr, one of America's outstanding theologians. It sounds impressive. But is it true? Apparently not. This does not *appear* to be the case.

I am not aware of "the question of faith" as I judge whether a minister should march. I do not inquire about the object of trust as I deliberate on the proper size of the welfare check. I do not struggle with the faith question as I struggle with foreign policy issues. Furthermore, even when I pull away from specific issues calling for particular moral judgments and ask the more general ethical question, I do not ask, "In what does man trust?" I ask, "What is the good?" or "What makes a right act right?" Moreover, when I read philosophical ethics, from Plato and Aristotle up to contemporary moralists, I find them dealing with the problems of the good and the right, principles and rules, norms and context—not the question of faith.

What, then, does Niebuhr—and the central Christian tradition for which he speaks here—mean by the declaration that the great ethical question is always the question of faith? On what grounds do Christians assert this?

The Question of Faith

The point can perhaps best be understood by examining what is meant by "the question of faith." Niebuhr suggests that the question of faith is an inquiry about the

You gotta believe
in something!

object of man's confidence: In what does man trust? I want to suggest some additional, complementary ways of posing this same question.

1. The question of faith is an inquiry into what makes life worth living for a person. Everyone who lives does so in the confidence that life is worth living, and such faith always depends on a prior confidence in something which gives life its worth. What is the object of that prior confidence? What does a person rely on to give meaning and value to his life? What means most to him? What does he count on to make it all worthwhile?

SAMPLE ANSWERS:

"I just live for my children."

"Pot, man, pot."

"I must maintain my integrity."

"Your smile makes it all worthwhile."

OTHER POSSIBLE ANSWERS: Sex. Money. The struggle for freedom, peace, and justice. God. A combination of the above.

A BIBLICAL EXAMPLE: The case of the rich young ruler (Luke 18:18-25). What meant most to him? How did his faith affect his behavior?

2. The question of faith asks what a man holds to as the ultimate criterion of right and wrong. Every moral judgment is made in light of some standard. A is right because of B. But why is B right? Because of C. But why is C right? Because . . . At the end of this chain of reasoning and justifications lies what one regards as the ultimate standard, that which is self-evidently good or right and which in the final analysis is the source of all other values—that which makes a right act right. One can affirm this final standard only in faith. He cannot prove that it is the final standard, because there is no higher standard by which to judge an ultimate standard. The question of faith: What does man hold as the ultimate standard of right and wrong?

SAMPLE ANSWERS:
"The Bible is the infallible rule for
    faith and practice."

"Mother said it was all right."

"My country, may she ever be right,
    but my country, right or wrong."

"It is for the greatest good of the
    greatest number."

OTHER POSSIBLE ANSWERS: The demands of justice. The teachings of the church. Love. God. A combination of the above.

A BIBLICAL EXAMPLE: The case of the unrecognized
truth (John 11:45-53). What was the standard
used in this judgment?

3. Faith means not only trust but also loyalty, not
only confidence but also commitment. In faith we rely
on that which gives value to us, and give allegiance to
that which we value. The question of faith: To what does
a man give his supreme allegience? When push comes to
shove, what does he hold on to? When the chips are
down, to what does he remain faithful?

SAMPLE ANSWERS:

"I love my country, but I love justice even more."

"For God, country, and Yale."

". . . to be thy loving and faithful husband,
as long as we both shall live."

"If you don't watch out for Number One, no one
else will."

OTHER POSSIBLE ANSWERS: The company. Mankind. Blacks. God.

A BIBLICAL EXAMPLE: The case of the overconfident
disciple (Matt. 26:30-35, 69-75). To what person or cause did this man express loyalty in
this incident?

4. Other versions of the question of faith: To whom
or what does a man feel ultimately accountable? To what
court does he make his final appeal? Whom does he seek
to please above all else?

SAMPLE ANSWERS:

"That's what you wanted me to do, isn't it, Mother?"

"I must obey my conscience."

"Don't blame me. I was ordered to do that."

"What do you fellows think?"

OTHER POSSIBLE ANSWERS: (Use your imagination.)

A BIBLICAL EXAMPLE: The case of the stouthearted men (Acts 5:21-32). To whom did they sense an ultimate obligation?

We've now looked at some different ways of raising the question of faith. Here are some findings from this examination:

1. Faith isn't intellectual assent to the truth of certain propositions, but a practical trusting in, relying on, giving of loyalty to, something.

2. All men, the unjust as well as the just, live by faith. They cannot help themselves. Even the man of great despair trusts that life with all its burdens is preferable to death—or he commits suicide.

3. The difference between the Christian and the non-Christian lies not in the fact that the former lives by faith while the latter does not, but in the fact that the Christian—to the degree that he *is* a Christian—relies on the God known in Jesus Christ, while his neighbor centers his life around some other object of ultimate concern.

4. Niebuhr was right. The great ethical question *is* the question of faith, because faith is the root and ground of all moral action. The direction of our loyalty and trust gives direction to every act we perform.

5. What counts is not what one *says* he trusts in, but what he actually relies on. "Not every one who says to me, 'Lord, Lord,' shall enter the kingdom of heaven . . ." (Matt. 7:21). What one counts on is revealed in his conduct. "You will know them by their fruits" (Matt. 7:20).

Let's consider now what difference a Christian's faith in God ought to make, can make, and sometimes does make in his moral life.[2]

What Is a Christian?

If you asked a contemporary churchman, "Are you a Christian?" you might receive any one of three answers:

Answer 1: Yes, I go to First Church.

Answer 2: Yes, I believe in Jesus Christ.

Answer 3: Well, I try to be.

Answer 1 indicates that being a Christian means *belonging* to a particular community of faith. Answer 2, that it involves *believing* in a certain Person. Answer 3, that it entails *behaving* in a certain way. All three answers are right.

Any one of them, of course, can go sour. Belonging can degenerate into just being on the church rolls. Believing can come to mean simply affirming five or fifteen or fifty fundamentals. And behaving can deteriorate into living by a legalistic code. Rightly understood, however, each answer stands, and the three stand together. Our concern right now is primarily with the effect of "believing" on "behaving." Consider for a moment, however, the importance of "belonging."

The Christian belongs. He is a member of that historical community of persons for whom Jesus Christ is central for both thought and action. One does not become a Christian and then join the church. In the very act of naming the name of Jesus in faith one asserts his membership in that community which calls Jesus Lord. There are many things that one can do alone, but being a Christian is not one of them. We cannot even know

Jesus Christ apart from the witness of Matthew, Mark, Luke, and John. And we surely cannot enter his company without also entering the company of Peter and Paul and James; of Augustine, Aquinas, and Francis; of Luther, Calvin, and Wesley; of Niebuhr, Tillich, and Pope John. Christian faith is always a personal faith, for, as Luther once observed, "Everyone must do his own believing, just as everyone must do his own dying." But the Christian's personal faith is always a shared faith, one he holds in common with all others in the fellowship.

The importance of the Christian's membership in the community of faith becomes clear when one recognizes that every type of human society—the family, the fraternity, the company, the nation—tends to generate its own *mores* or style of life, its own moral code or standard for living, and that each tends or attempts to impose that style and standard on its members. One is apt to hear at home, for example, "We don't do that in this family!" Or on the campus, "It's all right, man. Go ahead." Or in public life, "That's un-American!"

Every group to which we belong presses us to conform. And key groups are remarkably successful! When all the other guys at the shop hand out kickbacks, who am I to say that it is wrong? When all the gals in the garden club are horrified by my minister's marching, who am I to defend his action? When a whole society justifies systemic racial injustice, who am I to protest?

What the Christian faith has to offer in the face of this confusion of standards and conflicts of styles of life are the standards and styles of life of another group, the *koinonia,* the company of God's covenant people. Granted, you often can't tell the Christians from the lions without a scorecard. Granted, the church is not so much in the world as the world is in the church. Granted, "Men who love the Church always find it confusing and painful to contemplate the contradictions between the reality they love and the religious organizations which are called by the same name." [3] Granted all that. The fact remains that as long as I participate faithfully in this covenant community, I keep bumping into guys like Moses and Amos and Jeremiah. And Peter and Paul and John. And Calvin and Livingstone and Martin Luther King. And most of all, Jesus. They are my companions in this community. They set the styles and standards for this group. And at least some of their influence, the Lord willing, is bound to rub off.

What characterizes—or ought to characterize or can characterize—this group to which the Christian belongs is its faith in God. Christians are persons who through the ministry of Jesus Christ—his life, death, resurrection, and continuing presence in history—have come to trust in the Lord of heaven and earth. They rely on the one in whom all things live and move and have their being. They trust in him on whom all are utterly dependent. They count on his faithfulness, accept his forgiveness, and bank on his final victory. Christians, in a word, are people who through Jesus Christ have been given the great gift of confidence in the Almighty. The Christian knows that he is loved, accepted, forgiven, cared for by the Creator of the ends of the earth.

His faith, of course, is by no means perfect. Often he fears death, even though he has heard the promise of resurrection. Often he staggers under a burden of guilt, even though he has heard good news of God's forgiveness. Often he despairs in the face of man's inhumanity to man, even though he trusts that God rules over history. Every Christian encounters that mountain he cannot move, that crisis that arouses his suspicions, that tragedy that stirs distrust. The Christian, like his non-Christian neighbor, continually struggles with anxiety, despair, dread. It would be quite inaccurate to describe the Christian as a man of total or unqualified trust in God. A more accurate description maintains simply that a Christian—in the midst of his unbelief, helplessness, and self-love—has begun in some small measure to love, trust, and hope in God.

But faith, as we have seen, means not only trust but also loyalty, not only confidence in God's goodness but also commitment to God's cause. A Christian is thus one who with the help of Jesus Christ has heard and responded to not only the gospel but also the law. For him, both words come as the Word: "God loves you" *and* "Love God." "The kingdom of God is at hand" *and* "Seek first God's kingdom." "Come unto me" *and* "Deny yourself." Put another way, the Christian's faith is both active and passive. He receives in confidence; he acts in loyalty. He does not accept life as a gift from God without performing its duties. On the other hand, he does not perform life's duties apart from the confidence that he is sustained by grace. The Christian knows that the Word which confronts him expresses not only a gracious invitation to believe but also an inescapable call to obey. He knows further that he properly responds to the Word only when he both submits himself to God's law and finds security in God's love.

The Christian's commitment is no more perfect than his confidence is steadfast. Just as his faith is often mingled with distrust, so his loyalty is often corroded by disloyalty. If we reserve the name "Christian" only for those who have a Christlike devotion to God, then Jesus alone can bear the title. The mark of the Christian is not that he has attained the dedication of Christ, but that he has accepted such dedication as his standard. Not that he has fulfilled his obligations as a child of God, but that he has acknowledged them as *his* obligations. Not that he lives at all times as a citizen of God's kingdom, but that he seeks that kingdom above all else.

"Are you a Christian?"

"Well, I try to be."

The Life of Faith in God

What effect does such faith have on the moral life of the Christian? What is the impact of such believing on the way one behaves? Here are some differences which faith in God can make, ought to make, and sometimes does make in the life of the believer:

1. Faith in God as the one who in gracious love creates, sustains, governs, and forgives us moves the believer—in gratitude for such grace—to make a faltering response of reciprocal love. "We love, because he first loved us" (1 John 4:19). The believer knows that the purpose of the gospel is not simply that we should believe in the love of God but that we should return it. Faith in God's love toward man is perfected in our love for him and the neighbor.

The faithful life is thus the God-centered life. Its motive is the "expulsive power of a new affection"; its intention is to live to the praise of God's glory; its practice is the repeated, persistent presentation of one's self as "a living sacrifice, holy and acceptable to God" (Rom. 12:1). John Calvin indicated the basic posture of the Christian life in these words:

> We are not our own; therefore, neither is our own reason or will to rule our acts and counsels. We are not our own; therefore, let us not make it our end to seek what may be agreeable to our carnal nature. We are not our own; therefore, as far as possible, let us forget ourselves and the things that are ours. On the other hand, we are God's; let us, therefore, live and die to him. We are God's; therefore, let his wisdom and will preside over all our actions. We are God's; to him, then, as the only legitimate end, let every part of our life be directed. . . . Let this, then, be the first step, to abandon ourselves, and devote the whole energy of our minds to the service of God.[4]

2. Devotion to the service of God entails loyalty to the cause of God. The Bible describes that cause in various ways. Here it speaks of preparing for the kingdom; there, of reconciling the world. Here it is the healing of the nations; there, the freeing of the enslaved. Here the key word is justice; there, mercy. Here, righteousness; there, peace. The Christian knows that God calls him to heal the sick and clothe the naked, to visit the lonely and strengthen the weak, to seek the lost and help the helpless, to cast out demons and proclaim good news. The cause for which Christ enlists his allegiance and claims his loyalty has many facets and demands many gifts. No single statement can embrace it, no single principle convey it. Perhaps the least inadequate summary is that given by Paul: "For the whole law is fulfilled in one word, 'You shall love your neighbor as yourself' " (Gal. 5:14).

3. Faith as confidence in God to give meaning to one's life results in the freedom of the self. Apart from

such confidence, the self is apt to be enslaved. So great is the human need to be loved, wanted, cared for, accepted, that practically every man frantically tries to make a name for himself. In distrust of God we assume that if we do not justify our existence, life will be without meaning, value, and worth. Nowhere is this distrust more apparent than in the rigid orthodoxy of certain expressions of religion or in the excessive scrupulosity of legalistic morality.

But to the degree that we trust in God to give us value, we don't have to prove our worth. To the extent that we rely on his acceptance of us, we can drop our defenses. To the degree that we count on his word of promise, we can "sit loose" to everything else.

> Let goods and kindred go,
> This mortal life also;
> The body they may kill:
> God's truth abideth still;
> His Kingdom is forever.

Martin Luther's hymn is the song of a liberated man. Every Christian is entitled to sing it with wild abandonment. ". . . where the Spirit of the Lord is, there is freedom" (2 Cor. 3:17). "For freedom Christ has set us free . . . " (Gal. 5:1).

4. Faith in God as the center and source of all value prompts both protest and affirmation. Men of faith are incurable protesters. They protest against anything finite—nation, culture, mankind—that claims to be infinite; anything relative—mores, moral codes, ethical standards—that claims to be absolute; anything human—the self, the church, the in-group—that claims to be divine. Faith knows that God alone is God, that he alone

is holy. "You shall worship the Lord your God and him only shall you serve" (Matt. 4:10; cf. Deut. 6:13).

The counterpart of protest against idolatry is the affirmation of many relative values. Because God is the source and end of all things, whatever is, is good. It may be perverted, sinful, broken, but it is not bad, because God has made it and maintains it. "Everything is beautiful in its own way."

In faith the Christian accepts life in all its mystery as a great gift. He affirms himself, his sexuality, his color, his needs. He also affirms the neighbor, every neighbor, even the enemy neighbor, who though disvaluable to him is valuable to God. Faith moves the believer to an appreciation of the world and a desire to explore and understand it, to a profound sense of stewardship for all that is given, to tender loving care. "This is my Father's world." ". . . let us rejoice and be glad in it."

5. Faith in God as the final judge engenders in the believer a profound sense of personal responsibility to him. He is the Holy One "with whom we have to do" (Heb. 4:13). The moral life of the Christian is consciously lived before God, in relationship to him, in response to his present work in the world. The ultimate criterion of action is not what society says or reason demands or justice requires. The ultimate criterion is what *God* enables and requires one to do. The believer seeks to respond not so much to a law of love as to a loving Lord, not so much to principles and rules as to the God who reigns.

6. Finally, the Christian knows that because he is responsible to the Lord of heaven and earth, he has universal obligations.

To be responsible is to be able and required to give

account *to* someone *for* something. What a man is responsible for depends in part at least on the being to
whom he is accountable. Thus, if a man is accountable
only to his nation, then he is responsible only for his
fellow citizens and not for "gooks" or other foreigners.
If he responds only to the demands of some closed religious society, then he is answerable only for love of
the brethren, not for outsiders. If the God whom he
answers cares only for men's souls or spirits, the believer can neglect men's need for shoes and shelter. If
his God seeks only a more equitable distribution of this
world's goods, the believer can forget proclaiming the
gospel. If his God loves only individuals, the believer is
not accountable for social structures, public institutions,
or mankind as a whole. The scope of our responsibility
depends on the character of the one to whom we must
give account.

The Christian knows himself to be accountable to
the universal Lord. Before this Lord all nations are as
nothing; yet he marks the fall of even one tiny sparrow.
He has showed us what he requires: that we do justice
and love mercy and walk humbly with him. He has demonstrated how much he cares: he sent his only Son. He
has drafted us for his service: "Go and bear fruit." Because God is who he is, our obligations are unlimited.
"I am under obligation both to Greeks and to barbarians,
both to the wise and to the foolish" (Rom. 1:14).

QUESTIONS FOR THOUGHT AND DISCUSSION

1. The author suggests that some dimension of
faith is expressed in each of these biblical passages: Luke
18:18-25; John 11:45-53; Matthew 26:30-35, 69-75;
Acts 5:21-32. In what ways do you agree or disagree
with his interpretation?

2. Do you agree that "all men, the unjust as well as the just, live by faith"? Explain your answer.

3. What are some specific ways in which faith in one's nation as the ultimate giver of value or ultimate cause to live for would affect one's moral judgments?

4. How would you define "a Christian"? Compare your definition with the author's.

5. Comment: "The scope of our responsibility depends on the character of the one to whom we must give account."

6. Do you think differences in the ways Christians understand the responsibility of the church in society can be traced to differences in their understanding of what God's work in the world is? Why?

4 | PERCEPTIONS: What Do You See?

The frequency with which we use the phrase "He meant well, but . . ." demonstrates our awareness that even the most committed Christian sometimes makes a boo-boo. One possible reason: poor eyesight. In making judgments, we call them as we see them, and we often see them wrong. Observe:

Q. Is it morally permissible for a grown man to make a little child cry by sticking him with a needle?

A. It all depends.

Q. It all depends?

A. Yes. The action is wrong if the grown man is a sadist getting his kicks out of inflicting pain. It's okay if he is a physician giving a shot of penicillin.

Q. I see what you mean. But what if he is a physician who is also a sadist?

A. Move on to the next question, please.

Q. Is it right to help a man?

A. Yes.

Q. Even when he is robbing a bank?

A. No.

Q. Is it right to take food away from a hungry child?

A. No.

Q. Even when he is overeating?

A. Yes.

Our moral judgments depend both on how we interpret actions (what's the guy doing with that needle?) and on how we read the situations in which they take place (helping his friend do what?). Good eyesight is essential for responsible decision-making.

Jesus emphasized that. "Your eye is the lamp of your body," he said; "when your eye is sound, your whole body is full of light; but when it is not sound, your body is full of darkness" (Luke 11:34; see also Luke 4:18; 13:34; and 23:34).

In this chapter I want to mention some things that shape and influence our perceptions. We'll examine first some factors that seem to affect every man's perceptions, then suggest some ways faith in God can open your eyes.

Factors That Influence What We See

Five factors condition what we see: where we look from; whom we look with; what we look through; what we look at; and what we look for.

1. We are influenced by *where we look from*—that is, by our standpoint, our point of view. Things look different from the point of view of a child than from that of a parent. Blacks see America's racial crisis from one perspective, whites from another. Americans interpret the war in Southeast Asia from an American standpoint, the Vietcong from theirs. A twentieth-century man's viewpoint differs from that of a first-century man.

"Where we look from" refers to our location in society. All of us are located in various groups. My location, for example, is that of a white, middle-class, middle-aged, American, Christian clergyman in the ecclesiastical bureaucracy. This designation of my place indicates my race, socioeconomic class, age, nationality, occupation, and religious faith. Further designations of my location could include family status, political party, section of the country I come from, and the like.

Public opinion polls demonstrate dramatically how one's location in society—his race, age, class—influences what he sees, believes, feels, does, and judges to be right or wrong.

Item: A Louis Harris Survey in mid-1969 revealed

that only a narrow plurality of white people in America (46 to 43 percent) believed that Negroes were still discriminated against in the country. In contrast, blacks, by an overwhelming vote of 84 to 4 percent, said they *were* still discriminated against.[1]

Item: A national cross section of 1,885 individuals sixteen years of age and older were asked in mid-1969: "Do you tend to agree or disagree that the people running this country just don't want to listen to what young people have to say?" Young people, aged sixteen to twenty, agreed by 59 to 34 percent. "Old-timers," thirty-five to forty-nine years of age—you guessed it—disagreed, 54 to 33 percent.[2]

Item: Overwhelming agreement in the late 1960's came, it appears, only in disapproval by parishioners of their clergyman's participation in demonstrations! To this statement, "I would be upset if my (minister/priest/rabbi) were to participate in a picket line or demonstration," 72 percent of a national sample of laymen agreed. ("I *told* Tom Long he would make those people mad if he marched . . .") Even here, however, significant differences appeared in the different religious traditions. Agreement by religious group: Protestants, 77 percent; Catholics, 68 percent; Jews, 43 percent.[3]

Peter Berger, a sociologist worth his salt, indicates the impact of social conditioning on one's viewpoint, perceptions, attitudes, and style of life in these words:

> A sociologist worth his salt, if given two basic indices of class such as income and occupation, can make a long list of predictions about the individual in question even if no further information has been given. Like all sociological predictions, these will be

statistical in character. That is, they will be probability statements and will have a margin of error.
Nevertheless, they can be made with a good deal
of assurance. Given these two items of information
about a particular individual, the sociologist will be
able to make intelligent guesses about the part of
town in which the individual lives, as well as about
the size and style of his house. He will also be able
to give a general description of the interior decorat-
ing of the house and make a guess about the types
of pictures on the wall and books or magazines
likely to be found on the shelves of the living
room. Moreover, he will be able to guess what kind
of music the individual in question likes to listen
to. . . . He can predict which voluntary associations
the individual has joined and where he has his
church membership. He can estimate the individual's
vocabulary. . . . He can guess the individual's
political affiliation and his views on a number of
public issues. He can predict the number of children sired by his subject and also whether the latter
has sexual relations with his wife with the lights
turned on or off. . . . Finally, if the sociologist
should decide to verify all these guesses and ask the
individual in question for an interview, he can estimate the chance that the interview will be refused.[4]

2. What we see is influenced by *those whom we
look with* and what they report seeing—that is, by the
pressure of group opinions. This elaborates point 1.
There we said that our location in society conditions our
perceptions; here we tell why. All of us have a primeval
human urge to be accepted, to belong, to live in a world

with others. When everybody else is doing it or saying it· or seeing it, we are inclined to go along.

This is true even in our perception of physical objects. Social psychologists have conducted experiments which demonstrate the way in which group pressure affects perception even here. An individual confronted with an object that is, say, thirty inches in length will progressively modify his initially-correct estimate if placed in an experimental group all members of which keep insisting that they are quite sure that the thing is actually ten inches long.[5] If we yield to group pressure in our perception of even physical objects, how much more likely are we to yield as we seek to understand the *meaning* of something.

Our dependence on the reports of others becomes apparent to us when we get different signals from different groups to which we belong. The "credibility gap" developed in the mid-1960's because we got one version of the war in Vietnam from the White House, another from watching TV. Was the war in Vietnam a war of aggression by one nation against another—or a civil war of nationalists against the colonialists? Did the "body count" of "enemy killed" refer to armed soldiers—or women and children? Did the self-interest of the U.S. demand our involvement—or was the whole thing a tragic mistake? We kept getting different readings, and the question everyone asked was, Who can you believe?

Readers of Bill Buckley get one slant on the news; readers of Tom Wicker get another. *The Christian Century* reports events from one perspective, *Christianity Today* from another. Democrats tend to see political issues in one way, Republicans in another. The group we are in affects our eyesight. All of us have not only our location in society but also our reference groups—that is, groups whose opinions, convictions, and courses of action are decisive for the formation of our opinions, convictions, and courses of action.

3. What we see is shaped by *what we look through* —that is, by the "eyes" or "filters" growing out of our personal history, knowledge, experiences, imagination, desires, frustrations, and the like.

When I look at a situation, I look at it with my own eyes. These eyes are conditioned by my place in society: they are the eyes of a white, middle-class American. But they are also conditioned by everything which makes me different from other white, middle-class Americans: my unique experiences, my personality structure, my imagination and sensitivity.

Knowledge, experience, training, affect what we see. Thus the doctor sees things in the symptoms that the patient does not see. The lawyer sees possibilities for legal action that are not apparent to the non-lawyer. The teacher sees potentialities in the pupil which the student in his frustration cannot perceive.

Experiences of bereavement tend to increase our sensitivity to the feelings of others suffering grief. If we have been unjustly treated we are more likely to see how other victims of injustice feel. If our imagination and empathy are active, we can identify with others in their situations and say to them, "I see what you mean."

The state of one's health as well as the state of one's soul affects his perception and—therefore—his moral judgment. A father is much more likely to see his child's need for companionship late Saturday morning after a good night's rest than he is late Friday afternoon just after he's returned from an exhausting sales meeting in Atlanta.

4. What we see is conditioned by *what we look at*—that is, by the scope of our field of vision, by how we define the situation we are looking at, by what we regard as part of the context to be evaluated. James M. Gustafson makes the point effectively in his review of Joseph Fletcher's book *Situation Ethics:*

> If the situation is the determining factor in what love requires [as Fletcher contends], it is terribly important how one interprets his situation. In the interpretation, evaluations are already taking place. Is it boy plus girl between 1 A.M. and 3 A.M. after a number of drinks in a motel room who feel affection for each other stimulated by proper knowledge of erogenous zones? Or is it boy, responsible to others than the girl, and responsible to and for her over a long period of time under a covenant of some sort, plus girl concerned not only for the present moment but also for the past and future relationships, in a human community for whose vitality and order they have responsibility and which in turn has to seek its common good? The minimal facts may be the same: boy, girl, drinks, motel; the interpretation of what the situation *is* differs.[6]

What factors ought one to take into account as he evaluates U.S. policy in Vietnam? What constituted the situation at My Lai? How much history is the white man obligated to consider as he responds to a black demand for reparations? What factors—medical, legal, socio-economic, personal, moral—are relevant in a moral judgment about an abortion? One obviously cannot look at everything that has ever happened and everyone who has ever lived as he seeks to evaluate a particular action. One must draw the line somewhere. But where? How we assess a particular action will be greatly influenced by where we draw that line. What we see is conditioned by our field of vision.

5. What we see (and fail to see!) is influenced, finally, by *what we look for*—that is, by our self-interest or by what affects us most directly in the scene we are viewing. Self-interest, of which we are usually completely unaware, often blinds us to features in a situation which seem quite obvious to others and enables us to see features apparent to no one else. Popular wisdom acknowledges the operation of this factor through such sayings as these: "Love is blind." "I don't see what she sees in him." "That child has a face only a mother could love."

F. C. Sharp speaks of "spotlights" and "floodlights." [7] Often when we look at a situation, he says, we use spotlights, which bring certain features of the situation into clear visibility while placing others in a dim background. Instead, we ought to use floodlights.

As I write these words, the U.S. District Court in my area has just ordered the Richmond, Virginia, school board to achieve a unitary school system, even though this will require rather extensive crosstown busing. Everyone in town is talking about the court order. It is fascinating to observe what features of the order are "spotlighted" by different groups (depending primarily—once again—on their location in society).

Whites in Richmond are apt to highlight these undeniably true features of the court order: It means the end of the "freedom of choice" Richmond has operated with in recent years. It spells finis for neighborhood schools. It will require some children to ride buses for more than an hour each way, going right past much nearer schools. It will place some white children in schools that are overwhelmingly black. The Supreme Court has not yet ruled on whether busing is mandatory if this is the only way a school can achieve a unitary system.

Blacks, on the other hand, are apt to focus their spotlights on these equally undeniable features of the situation: The *Brown v. Board of Education* ruling of the Supreme Court which declared segregation in the public schools to be unconstitutional was issued way back in 1954, for pity's sake. Richmond's so-called freedom-of-choice plan has resulted in 75 percent of the Richmond schoolchildren being in racially identifiable schools. Busing isn't totally unheard of: last year, 10,000 schoolchildren rode buses. We don't normally wait until the Supreme Court has made a ruling before we obey the order of a lower court.

Psychologists call this "selective perception." Sharp is surely right when he says we ought to look at situations with floodlights, not spotlights, so that we can see every feature that needs to be taken into account. The fact remains, however, that it is extremely difficult for us to take our eyes off those features of a situation which affect us and ours most directly.

The Effect of Faith

How does, can, or ought faith in the God and Father of our Lord Jesus Christ affect what we see? Five possibilities:

1. Faith does not remove us from our location in society, but it does add a new place from which to look: the vantage point of a child of God. The perspective I have as one who knows himself accountable to the universal Lord of heaven and earth does not replace all other

perspectives, but it does or can or ought to check and
correct them. By faith I ought to always and sometimes
do look at situations not only as a white, middle-class,
middle-aged American, but as a white, middle-class,
middle-aged American who is also a Christian. If I believe that my race, class, age, and nationality affect me
no longer, I deceive myself and the truth is not in me
(cf. 1 John 1:8). But if I recognize the impact that my
place in society has on my interpretations of what is
going on, that impact is usually somewhat softened.

2. Precisely the same point can be made in regard
to self-interest. Faith in Jesus Christ checks self-interest.
Obviously it does not free one completely from that in-
ordinate self-love which is incompatible with the divine
will. As Reinhold Niebuhr has observed:

> The sorry annals of Christian fanaticism, of unholy
> religious hatreds, of sinful ambitions hiding behind
> the cloak of religious sanctity, of political power
> impulses compounded with pretensions of devotion
> to God, offer the most irrefutable proof of the error
> in every Christian doctrine and every interpretation
> of the Christian experience which claim that grace
> can remove the final contradiction between man and
> God. The sad experiences of Christian history show
> how human pride and spiritual arrogance rise to
> new heights precisely at the point where the claims
> of sanctity are made without due qualification.[8]

Yet when one makes "due qualification," he can say
that faith in Jesus Christ can and sometimes does break
at least part of the hold of self-interest on the Christian,
so that he is able on occasion to look at situations not
only in terms of what they mean to him and his loved

ones or nation or race, but also in terms of what they mean to other men, other nations, other races.

3. Faith in Jesus Christ can, ought to, and sometimes does affect how the Christian defines the situation. The Christian knows, for example, that God is an interested party in every situation and that in all his dealings he must deal with God. The Christian knows, moreover, that because God is universal he (the Christian) has obligations to all men. Such self-awareness provides no easy answer to the question of where one draws the line in defining a situation to be judged. But that, perhaps, is its chief value. The awareness that we are universally responsible to the universal Lord who loves all that he has made ought to engender a healthy skepticism about all easy answers (our own and those of our companions) and ought furthermore to prompt prophetic protest against unduly narrow definitions of that for which we are accountable.

4. Faith, finally, ought to, can, and sometimes does give to the Christian not only a new sense of the scope of the situation but also a new sensitivity to certain features in that situation. The God to whom the Christian is committed is clearly "biased" in favor of the weak, the poor, the outcast, the rejected. He sees the affliction of the afflicted; he hears the cry of those in need. (See, for example, Exodus 3:7-8; Psalm 107:41; Isaiah 36:9.) Moreover, in the parable of the last judgment Jesus has so identified himself with the hungry, the thirsty, the naked, the sick, the prisoner, that ministry to one of the least of these his brethren is ministry to him (Matt. 25:31-46). Allegiance to Jesus ought to and occasionally does open the eyes of his followers to Christ's claim in the claim of the neighbor, to opportunities to glorify God in the least expected places.

We dare not claim too much. The situation is not "Once I was blind, but now I see." Faith in Christ does not guarantee unprejudiced perceptions. We are not completely healed. Our condition is more like that of the blind man who, when first touched by Jesus, had to report, "I see men; but they look like trees, walking" (Mark 8:24). We do not see everything clearly. But, by grace, some things are beginning to move.

QUESTIONS FOR THOUGHT AND DISCUSSION

1. The author identifies five factors which condition what we see. Can you think of some others? Which factor influences our perception most?

2. Several questions are raised on page 57 about what factors one ought to take into account as he evaluates U.S. policy in Vietnam, the black demand for reparations, or an abortion. Review these questions. How would you answer them?

3. Select some controversial issue now in the news —a bill before Congress, a recent Supreme Court ruling, some government policy—and gather different interpretations of that issue from different newspapers and/or columnists. Try to get clippings from white and black papers, regular and underground papers.

a. What features of the issue are spotlighted in each clipping? What ignored?

b. What basic assumptions are made but not specified?

c. Which interpretation of the facts seems most accurate to you? Which most biased? Why?

4. Identify at least one issue on which each pair of the following groups are likely to have different percep-

tions, and summarize what the different interpretations of that issue are likely to be:

    a. Radical students and the university administration
    b. Democrats and Republicans
    c. Blacks and whites
    d. Protestants and Roman Catholics

5. Can you give an example of something that you now see in a way different from the way you saw it a decade ago? What effected the change in your perception?

5 | PRINCIPLES:
How Do You Tell Right from Wrong?

Most moral judgments come easy to us. We carry around our moral rules, maxims, guidelines, principles; we see situations where they fit easily; we make our judgment. Example:

SITUATION: I have promised my wife that I will dry the dishes tonight, but here I sit watching "Laugh-In" on TV. The rattling noise my wife is making as she washes the dishes (My, how those dishes are rattling!) reminds me of my promise which, regrettably, had temporarily slipped my mind.

MORAL PRINCIPLE: One ought to keep his promises.

MORAL JUDGMENT: I ought to get up from here this very moment and go dry those dishes— and I will do so as soon as the next commercial comes on. (Confidential memo to self: Be more careful in making promises from now on.)

If all moral judgments came as easy as that one, moral judgment-making would be a breeze. But, of course, they don't, and it isn't. Sometimes the moral rules and principles we live by clash with one another and we feel a conflict of obligations. What do we do in such a situation? Normally we try to formulate a new moral rule for ourselves which in some way recognizes the binding character of both obligations we feel. Often this attempt to make a new moral rule is successful. But sometimes it fails, and we find that we simply cannot meet all the moral claims which press in upon us.

So what do we do then? We make an extremely difficult moral choice: We acknowledge one claim as more binding on us than the other, and we meet the obligations of that more binding claim, even though doing so involves violating the obligations of the other. The fateful choice we make in such a situation reveals our underlying theory of ethics, that is, our basic assumption about what makes a right act right. Many of us are not even aware of what theory of ethics we hold to until we are confronted with an agonizingly difficult moral dilemma.

A Case Study: Moral Judgments About the War in Vietnam

Thousands of Americans found themselves in such a moral dilemma in the mid-1960's as they tried to make responsible judgments about their nation's policy in Vietnam. Was it morally right or wrong for America to participate in that war? Equally sincere Americans gave different answers to that question, and both defenders and critics of U.S. policy offered persuasive moral arguments. Let's now examine, as a case study in moral reasoning, some of those moral arguments offered by the Johnson administration and its critics in the mid-1960's, setting aside for this purpose more recent discussion about U.S. policy in Southeast Asia. Such an examination of the early Vietnam debate ought to illuminate other debates on public policy, as well as shed light on less critical judgments we make every day about what is right or wrong.

The Problem: Moral Rules in Conflict

One of the basic arguments in support of U.S. policy

in Vietnam was that we had a promise to keep. President
Johnson expressed the argument like this in his Johns
Hopkins address on April 7, 1965:

> We are there because we have a promise to
> keep. Since 1954 every American President has of-
> fered support to the people of South Viet-Nam. . . .
> To dishonor that pledge, to abandon this small and
> brave nation to its enemies, and to the terror that
> must follow, would be an unforgivable wrong.[1]

Critics dealt with that argument in any one (or all)
of three ways. Some denied its factual premise. Eisenhower's promise to Diem in 1954, they said, was—as
Eisenhower himself later explained—a pledge for foreign
aid, not for a military program. Kennedy had indicated
support, but he had also said, "We can help them, we can
give them equipment, we can send our men out there as
advisers, but they have to win it—the people of Vietnam
—against the Communists." Moreover, the promise had
been made to a regime we ourselves had installed, "our
own agent" as it were; so the promise was not really
binding.

A second ploy of critics was to lessen the impact of
the promise by questioning some assumptions often cited
with it. President Johnson, some critics contended, was
simply making an emotional appeal by referring to a
"terror that must follow." On what grounds did he declare that terror would follow American withdrawal? On
what grounds did he judge the potential terror of the
future worse than the present terror and destruction cre-
ated by our military machine?

The principal response of critics to the claim of the
promise-keeping rule, however, was neither to deny the

I am a man of my word.

validity of the pledge nor to try to lessen its impact. The principal response was to show (or try to show!) that in this particular circumstance another rule was more binding. A rule frequently cited as more binding was one drawn from the traditional and widely accepted definition of a "just war": one ought not to make deliberate, direct attacks on noncombatants.

Citing this rule, which protects prisoners of war

and civilians in civilized conflict, critics of U.S. policy charged that our conduct of the war—particularly our bombing of villages in "free strike" zones—constituted a crime so grave as to outweigh the binding character of our promise or the political consequences of a radical change of policy. Peter Berger, who called himself a political conservative and who acknowledged the validity of some of the political arguments offered by the Administration such as the "domino theory," expressed the argument like this:

> The terrible fact about our engagement in Vietnam is that it entails crime. . . .
>
> . . . we have reached a point where morality must take precedence over politics in any proper evaluation of the Vietnamese situation. The moral principle that must now become primary is that a major crime is to be condemned, *even if it should turn out to be part of a policy that is not a mistake.*
>
> . . . *The crime consists of waging a war that, by its very methods and routine manner, involves the killing of large numbers of helpless people.*
>
> . . . The intrinsic logic of this war has led to the dropping of napalm on children. Precisely at this point *political* argumentation becomes not only irrelevant but indecent.[2]

Some men tried to lessen the force of Berger's argument in any one or all of three ways. Some charged that figures indicating civilian victims of napalm and other casualties were exaggerated. Others commented, "War is hell." Still others, such as Paul Ramsey, contended that our bombing policy was not a violation of the rule of noncombatant immunity (also called the principle of discrimination). Said Ramsey, a widely recognized authority on the meaning of the "just war doctrine":

> I myself have no hesitation in saying that the counter-insurgency in South Vietnam in its chief or central design falls within the principle of discrimination. It is directed upon combatants as these have organized themselves for war, i.e., among the people like fish in water. No Christian and no moralist should assert that it violates the moral immunity of non-combatants from direct, deliberate attack to direct the violence of war upon vast Vietcong strongholds whose destruction unavoidably involves the collateral deaths of a great many civilians.[3]

However, assume for a moment—for our purposes here:

(1) that Berger was correct and that our method of conducting the war violated the moral rule declaring that noncombatants are morally immune from direct, deliberate attack;

(2) that the only way to keep our promise to South Vietnam was to conduct war in this rule-violating manner; and

(3) that President Johnson was correct in his assumption that to dishonor our pledge would be to abandon a small and brave nation to a terror that would follow.

Where does this set of assumptions leave the conscientious judgment maker? In a bind, naturally! One rule to which he assents, which we will call Rule A, says, "Keep your promises." Another, which we will call Rule B, says, "Don't kill civilians." What do you do when caught between two conflicting rules?

One Possible Solution: Creating a More Inclusive Rule

What we normally try to do in such a situation is to elevate the two rules into a more inclusive one which recognizes the binding character of both demands. Frederick S. Carney illustrates the procedure like this:

> . . . suppose there is a valid rule that I should not turn my back on my son when he especially needs help, and another that I should not enter the classroom as a teacher without being adequately prepared. It takes little imagination to conceive the details of a conflict between such obligations to family and vocation. The solution to this type of situation (and the one we quite naturally apply when confronted with such conflicts) is to elevate both rules into a new and more inclusive one in which we attempt to meet over the course of time our obligations in each area, and yet set forth the conditions under which our attention at any given time is to be granted primarily to one or to the other.[4]

The new rule regulating policy in Vietnam, for example, would be: keep your promises in ways that do not violate the moral immunity of noncombatants from direct, deliberate attack.

For purposes of illustration we have assumed that this solution is not possible. We have assumed that the only way to keep our promise is to kill noncombatants. The situation we have assumed is by no means an unreal one. Often we find that we simply cannot combine the two rules in such a nice and neat way. The man hiding Jews in his attic could protect them only by lying to the Gestapo at the door. He couldn't say to himself, "Protect Jews in ways that do not involve lying," or "Always tell the truth, but in ways that do not endanger Jews hiding in your attic."

A Second Possible Solution: Creating a
Rule with an Exception

If we can't combine the two rules, what do we do? We accept one as more binding on us in that particular situation or sort of situation, and make a new rule with an exception built in. Your new rule, depending on which of the original rules you regarded as more binding, would read as one of the following:

> Rule A-modified: "Always keep your promises, *except* when to do so would involve killing noncombatants."

> Rule B-modified: "Never kill noncombatants, *except* when to do so is required in order to keep a promise."

Rule A-modified obviously gives priority to the noncombatant rule, Rule B-modified to the promise-keeping one. The question now is, On what basis is the preference to be made? Is "not killing noncombatants" more valuable or more binding than "keeping your word"? Or ought one to keep his promises regardless of consequences?

Let us assume, for the sake of continuing our examination of rules, that on the grounds that "people are more important than promises," one chooses Rule A-modified, which calls for promise-keeping in ordinary circumstances, yet justifies the breaking of a promise if such violation is necessary in order to avoid attacking noncombatants. If all we had to contend with were these two rules we'd be in fairly good shape. But look back at the third assumption we accepted for purposes of this examination: by failing to attack noncombatants we abandon a small and brave nation to terror. In other words, if we follow Rule A-modified, and refuse to kill noncombatants, the consequences for the South Vietnamese people will be disastrous.

The Fateful Choice

The issue before us now is: What does the conscientious man do when compliance with a valid moral rule ("Do not conduct direct, deliberate attacks on noncombatants") will surely result in evil consequences (the terror that would befall the South Vietnamese if we quit bombing those villages)? One's options in this dilemma seem distressingly limited to two:

OPTION X: One can hold fast to the rule regardless of its consequences. Berger seems to be choosing this option: "The intrinsic logic of this war has led to the dropping of napalm on children. Precisely at this point *political* argumentation becomes not only irrelevant but indecent."

OPTION Y: One can hold fast to the desired consequences and affirm his readiness to do anything necessary to realize this end. In terms of our example, one who chooses this option might say: "Sure, bombing the VC-controlled villages occasionally results in the death of some women and children. I regret that very much. But if we didn't drop those bombs, Charlie would control Saigon by next week, and that would be disastrous for all of us, but especially for the South Vietnamese who have thrown their lot in with us. Recall how many people the Reds executed when they came to power in Hanoi. Remember that almost a million Catholics 'voted with their feet' after the Geneva Accords by coming south from Hanoi-controlled territory. And don't forget all the assassinations the Reds committed at Hue. We simply can't let that happen again. War is hell, and lots of women and kids get hurt. But we've got to do it."

The man who chooses Option X assumes—whether he recognizes it or not—the *duty* theory of ethics. He holds that there are some acts which are so wrong by their very nature that the morally responsible man cannot do them under any circumstances. For this man, nothing could justify dropping napalm on kids.

The person who chooses Option Y operates—knowingly or not—with the *results* theory of ethics. He assumes that the single obligation in the moral life is to do good, by which he means, to produce valuable results. If a particular act is necessary for the sake of the desired consequences, so be it. Ends justify means. One must do what is required for the sake of the cause. Even if it is necessary—for the sake of preventing the fall of Saigon—to napalm VC-controlled villages in which there may be children, it is our moral obligation to do precisely that.

We will examine these two theories of ethics, plus a third one, in the next chapter. Meanwhile, note that the issue between those who hold that some acts are always morally forbidden, and those who contend that we must always do what will result in the greatest good, crops up all over the place. Here are three examples:

EXAMPLE 1: The nuclear deterrence theory contends that all-out nuclear war has been avoided because of the mutual balance of terror. Each side knows that the other could destroy it in a retaliatory move, so the temptation to make a first strike is lessened. The threat deters because it is credible. We have let the Soviet Union know that we would not hesitate to destroy it if it attacked us first.

Advocates of results eithics contend that this good end of avoiding a nuclear war justifies the threat of destroying millions of Soviet men, women, and children. Inquiry raised by certain duty-ethics supporters: Would *you* be willing to push the button? Could you justify destroying millions of human beings simply in retaliation? If not, are you willing for your government to be prepared to push the button? To which certain results-ethics people reply: Okay, fellow. If you are not willing to push the button yourself or to allow our government to be ready to do so, are you prepared to engage in unilateral disarmament . . . and are you prepared to sit by and watch what the Communists would surely do if we didn't have the Bomb ready to go off if needed?

EXAMPLE 2: Under what conditions, if any, is it proper to violate the rights of free speech and free press in order to protect the public from pornography?

EXAMPLE 3: If the government could break the power of the Black Panthers and put a quietus on ghetto-rioting by killing ten Black Panther leaders, would it be justified in doing so? How about framing ten leaders instead of killing them? How about three instead of ten? Would you be willing for the government to frame one innocent man if by so doing it could in all probability prevent a race riot in which hundreds of persons might be killed or wounded?

QUESTIONS FOR THOUGHT AND DISCUSSION

1. In what ways—if any—do you find valid this chapter's description of how we use moral rules in judgment-making? What are your basic criticisms of this description?

2. Assuming the situation described in the chapter, would you choose Option X or Option Y on page 72 ? Why?

3. Where do you stand on the questions raised in Examples 1, 2, and 3 at the end of the chapter?

4. Identify and comment on two additional social problems in which there emerges the issue between those who hold that some acts are always wrong and those who hold that we must do whatever is necessary to produce the greatest good.

6 | PRINCIPLES: What Makes an Act Right?

All moral judgments are made on the basis of some moral standard. We call an act right and feel free or obligated to do it if it measures up to our standard; we call it wrong and morally forbidden if it violates our standard. A moral standard, we suggested in chapter 2, consists of a very loosely organized and only partially articulated collection of moral principles and rules, attitudes and feelings, commitments and faith.

Undergirding every moral standard is a basic assumption about what makes a right act right. We are calling that basic assumption a theory of ethics. Everybody has one floating around somewhere.

Often we are not aware of what theory of ethics we operate with. One reason: our theory seems so self-evident to us that we have never examined it. For instance, we wonder who could possibly question that what makes an act right is that it results in the most possible good in that situation. Everybody knows that! Another reason many of us are not aware of the theory we assume: our everyday moral judgments are made not on the basis of the theory itself, but on the basis of much more tangible and familiar principles and rules. Why worry about a theory of ethics when we've got plenty of rules and principles to guide us? We usually know what we ought to do.

Sometimes, however, as we saw in the last chapter, we are not sure what we ought to do. Our moral rules and principles so conflict that we must make a fateful choice between their claims. The choice we make in such a situation reveals what our basic theory of ethics really is. Because few of us are completely consistent, we may discover that we assume one theory in some circumstances and another in other circumstances.

What theory of ethics do you operate with? Probably one of the three basic theories current in Western society today. Practically everyone in our culture assumes one (or more!) of these theories. We identified two of them in chapter 5 as the *duty* theory and the *results* theory. The third is the *responsibility* theory. In this book, I am calling persons who assume these theories duty-ethicists, results-ethicists, and responsibility-ethicists, whether such persons are moral philosophers or theologians who advocate these theories or ordinary laymen who use them, knowingly or not.

In this chapter, I want to examine these three theories of ethics and indicate some of the values and problems of each. In the next chapter we'll look at some of the Christian versions of these theories. Each of the three theories of ethics, whether in its secular or Christian version, is based on or associated with a fundamental assumption about what man is like in his moral life.[1] We'll begin with one of those assumptions.

Man the Maker: Results Theories of Ethics

What is man like in his moral life? Some people assume that he is like a *maker*, a craftsman, a builder who constructs things according to an ideal for the sake of a goal. How does a woman go about making a cake? She gets a vision of the cake in mind, and then mixes the proper ingredients, flour, yeast, milk, eggs, salt, pepper—whatever goes into a cake—in order to realize or actualize that vision. Our moral life is like that, according to this central tradition. It consists of choosing ends or goals or purposes, and then doing those things which move us toward the selected goal. Particular moral judgments are made in light of these visions, dreams, ideals, purposes, objectives, goals. What we aim for provides the standard for judging what we are to do: Will this particular action help realize the desired goal?

Ethical theories which hold that the moral quality of an act is determined by its results are *results* theories. (The more technical name is *teleological* theories, from the Greek word meaning "the science of ends.") We encountered results-ethicists in the dramatic sketch with which this book began; they were those who praised or condemned their pastor's participation in the welfare demonstration because of its good or bad consequences. We saw them in our examination of the Vietnam debate (chapter 5) in those who defended U.S. involvement in that war on the grounds that a withdrawal would result in disastrous consequences for South Vietnam, our nation, and the peace and security of the free world. William Frankena summarizes the common conviction of all results-ethicists in these words:

> . . . an act is *right* if and only if it or the rule under which it falls produces, will probably produce, or is intended to produce *at least as great a balance of good over evil* as any available alternative; an act is *wrong* if and only if it does not do so. An act *ought to be done* if and only if it or the rule under which it falls produces, will probably produce, or is intended to produce *a greater balance of good over evil* than any available alternative.[2]

Results-ethicists differ among themselves over two questions:

1. *What* is the good one ought to seek in all his actions? For example, hedonists (from the Greek word meaning "pleasure") say that pleasure is the good we are to seek in everything, and conclude that the right course of action is that which produces at least as great a balance of pleasure over pain as any alternative would. Other results-ethicists contend that the good we ought to seek in everything is power, knowledge, self-realization, eternal life, the vision of God, moral integrity, peace, freedom, justice, or something else.

2. *Whose* good ought one to seek? Ethical egoism holds that one ought always to promote his own greatest good (whatever the good is—pleasure, power, integrity, etc.). Ethical universalism—often called utilitarianism—contends that we ought always to produce the greatest possible balance of good over evil in the universe as a whole, or "the greatest good for the greatest number."

Here are some typical results-ethics statements you are likely to hear any day:

> "For the sake of our kids, we've got to crack down on smut peddlers."

> "The peace and security of the free world depend upon America's determination and power to contain Communism."

> "Have a drink. It'll do you good."

Man the Citizen: Duty Theories of Ethics

A second basic tradition in ethics says that in our moral life we are not so much like craftsmen as we are like *citizens,* persons living under law. In craftsmanship both the ends and the means are relatively under our control. But the moral life isn't so simple! What we recognize when we reflect on our moral experience is that from infancy on we are surrounded, permeated, bombarded, floored, and flooded with all sorts of rules, commandments, directions, orders, laws. "Eat your spinach." "Don't drive over 60." "Quit hitting your sister." "Visit the dentist." "That's a no-no." "Pay your taxes." "Love your neighbor." "Make a profit." "Get some exercise." "Go to church." The difficulty in moral judgment-making, according to this tradition, lies not in deciding which end to aim at but in determining which law to obey. "What shall I do?" means "Which claim shall I yield to?"

Theories of ethics based on this model of man in his moral life are *duty* theories. (The technical name is *deontological* theories, from the Greek words meaning "the science of obligation or duty.") Two things characterize such theories. One is the contention that the moral value of acts or the moral rules they fall under depends on something other than the results they produce or are expected or intended to produce. Results-ethicists, we have seen, contend that the right is determined by results: if an act promotes more good than any alternative act could in those circumstances, it is the right act. Duty-ethicists deny what results-ethicists affirm. There are, they say, at least other considerations which may make an act or rule right or wrong besides the goodness or badness of its consequences. It may be, for example, that a particular act is right because it keeps a promise, because it is legal, because it is just, or because God commands it. In other words, I may be obli-

gated to do something—to tell the truth, for instance—
even though it does not promote the greatest possible
balance of good over evil.

A second characteristic of most duty theories is the
contention that the validity of moral rules or of acts based
on them lies in their conformity to universal and eternal
moral laws. Many advocates of a duty theory contend,
in addition, that certain acts are always and under any
conditions right in themselves (e.g., telling the truth),
and others are always and under any conditions wrong in
themselves (e.g., rape).

Advocates of both results ethics and duty ethics (as well as advocates of the ethics of responsibility) use moral rules and principles. Their difference lies in the theory which justifies the principle. Both, for example, could hold that one ought to keep his promises. The results-ethicist would justify this on the grounds that promise-keeping ordinarily results in the most good for society; the duty-ethicist, on the grounds that it is the nature of a promise that once you have made one, you are obligated to keep it.

Both theories, moreover, might provide grounds for breaking a promise. The results man might say, for example, that in this particular situation, one could do more good by breaking a promise than by keeping it; the duty man, that in a particular situation, another obligation (such as the obligation of children to care for their aged parents) might be more binding than the usually-binding obligation to keep your promise. The duty-ethicist would say, for example, that even though you promised the boys you'd go bowling with them tonight, if your mother has a heart attack, you ought to take her to the hospital rather than go bowling, because in that situation your duty to your mother is more binding. The results-ethicist would justify the trip to the hospital rather than to the bowling alley on the grounds that it did more good. (Decisions are easy when both theories agree. It's when they differ that we are faced with a moral dilemma.)

Man the Answerer: Responsibility Theories of Ethics

The third great symbol or image of man in his moral life is *man the answerer,* man the responder. What are we like in our practical moral existence as deciding, choosing, acting beings? We are like a man answering questions addressed to him, or a person defending himself against attack, or a man replying to appeals or meeting challenges. Another image: In our moral life we are like an automobile driver who must make forty decisions a minute. A driver's conduct cannot be adequately explained in terms of either his intended destination or his obedience to the rules of the road. His action is responsive action which is governed by what he sees other drivers on the road and children on the sidewalk doing, and by his anticipation of what they will do next.

So it is in our moral life. As we struggle with what we ought to do in any serious or novel situation, we are conscious not so much of goals and ideals, or of laws and commandments, as we are of people, powers, needs, relationships, changes, movements, happenings. Our moral concern and obligation is to respond in a fitting way to what is happening, to do the suitable or appropriate thing. The moral question "What shall I do?" is really the question "What is the fitting thing for me to do in this situation?"

A theory of ethics based on this image of man in his moral life is an *ethics of responsibility*. Such a theory contends that what makes a right act right is that it is the fitting act, the appropriate thing to do in that particular context, the act that most suitably responds to the reality of that situation. Such a theory would hold, for example, that the reason it was morally proper for the man of our illustration to break his promise to go bowling in order to rush his mother to the hospital was that this was the fitting thing to do, given that situation.

The three basic theories can be summarized and compared like this:

Results theories contend that an act is right if and only if that act will result or will probably result in more good than any other act would. "What shall I do?" means "What is most likely to result in the most good?" The problems for a results-ethicist in telling right from wrong lie in (1) determining what good he is aiming at for whom, and (2) deciding what action would probably produce the hoped-for results.

Duty theories contend that an act is right if and only if it conforms to the real moral law. "What shall I do?" means "Which claim or obligation shall I fill?" The basic problems in moral discernment for a duty-ethicist are (1) deciding which moral rules or principles are valid expressions of the universal moral law, and (2) deciding how to "apply" those valid moral principles to the situation at hand.

Responsibility theories hold that an act is right if and only if it is fitting action, one that fits into a total and dynamic situation as response to prior action and as anticipation of further response: "What shall I do?" means "What is the most suitable thing for me to do?" The questions which the responsibility-ethicist must answer as he seeks to discern what is fitting are: What is going on? Who is involved? To whom am I responsible for what?

Perhaps you now recognize which theory of ethics you operate with. You may have been a results-ethicist all these years without knowing it!

Some Strengths and Weaknesses of Each Theory

Which theory makes the most sense? Is it our fundamental obligation in every situation to do whatever is most likely to produce the best results? Is it to comply with a universal moral law, regardless of consequences? Or is it to do whatever best fits into that situation? Every man must answer for himself. I indicate my answer and the reasons for it in the next chapter. Here I'll simply suggest some of the strengths and weaknesses in each theory.

There is surely much to commend in the *results-ethicist's* concern for consequences. Sometimes, it seems, it is necessary to tell a lie in order to save the Jews in the attic, or to break the speed limit in order to get the patient to the hospital, or—most people believe—to go to war for the sake of justice. Most moral rules do seem to be guidelines, not ironclad laws; illuminators of our path, not holy commandments. People are more important than principles, promises, or precepts. In every situation we ought to ask, "What act will do the most good here?" Holders of this theory have much to teach us. They, however, are not entirely free from all difficulties. Here are some questions for them:

1. How do you measure the consequences of an act? Over what period of time? For whom must the consequences be good?

2. How much good must one be able to do in order to justify breaking a moral rule, such as the one regarding promises?

3. What consequences are you talking about—intended and expected results or actual results? If the intended consequences are good but the actual results disastrous, is the act right or wrong?

4. Are you prepared to say that a good end justifies *any* means? To return to our case study from the previous chapter, does protecting the life and freedom of the South

Vietnamese people justify U.S. military involvement in Vietnam? Does it justify bombing Vietcong-controlled villages even when this involves dropping napalm on women and children? How about torturing Vietcong prisoners of war in order to make them reveal military secrets? How about torturing their children before their eyes if this is the only way to make them talk?

Note that if the advocate of results ethics draws the line at any particular act ("I don't mind dropping napalm on kids, but I'm not about to pull out anybody's finger-nails"), he is no longer a consistent advocate of the position that "stopping Communism justifies any means necessary." Instead, he has switched over to the duty-ethicist's position, though the moral rule he is going to follow regardless of the consequences prohibits, for example, face-to-face torture rather than dropping napalm from ten thousand feet up in the air. His position now is: "I don't care what happens to Saigon, Singapore, or San Francisco. I am not going to torture a fellow human being."

The *duty-ethicist* also has much to commend in his position. He takes moral obligations with great serious-ness. He is particularly sensitive to the character of moral acts; he holds that there are some acts, such as promise-keeping, which by their very nature lay undeniable demands on us, and there are other acts, such as torturing a fellowman, which are so repulsive that no morally responsible person could do them under any circumstances. Scorned by his critics as a "legalist," he is in fact a "man of principle." The problems facing him seem to be these:

1. Which rules or principles are absolutely inviolable? Are *all* moral rules absolute? If not, how do you tell "moral laws" from "rules of thumb"?

2. How do you avoid legalism? Not every man of principle is a legalist, but every one is in danger of becoming a legalist. A legalist—by my loaded definition—is a man whose *primary* concern in the moral life is to obey the right moral law and thereby keep himself morally clean, pure, and guiltless.

3. Are you sensitive enough to the neighbor? A duty-conscious boy scout can be so intent on keeping himself physically strong, mentally awake, and morally straight that he doesn't see the sweet old lady on the corner who needs help in crossing the street.

The *responsibility-ethicist* seems to play the moral game by ear. This doesn't mean that he fails to take his moral obligation seriously. On the contrary, his passion is to act appropriately. But he does play it loose. He brings no prefabricated answers to his judgment-making situations. Instead, he tries to analyze every situation carefully, to be as sensitive as possible to what's going on, to figure out as best he can what's likely to happen next—and then to make a judgment about what sort of response is called for. The person who feels an obligation to do the fitting thing in every situation usually manages to avoid the legalism which tempts his duty-ethics companion and the good-ends-justify-any-means trap of his results-ethics companion. Some questions which he doesn't easily avoid are these:

1. What does the mandate to do the "fitting" thing involve? The obligation to "produce good results" is clear; the duty to "obey the moral law" is clear. The call to "act appropriately" seems awfully fuzzy.

2. How in the world do you tell "what's going on"? The slogan is catchy, but what does it mean? What safeguards do you have against misreading a situation?

3. Even if you manage to read the situation rightly, how do you decide what act fits in? What are your criteria for measuring whether an act is suitable?

So much for our exploration of traditional theories of ethics. Where—you are surely asking by now—do Christians stand on these issues? What is the Christian theory of ethics?

Read on.

QUESTIONS FOR THOUGHT AND DISCUSSION

1. What reasons might advocates of the three theories of ethics give in support of these moral rules or principles?

   a. A man ought always do what he feels he ought to do.
   b. Sex outside of marriage is wrong.
   c. Children should honor their parents.
   d. In a democracy, no one has the right to engage in civil disobedience.

2. On what grounds might advocates of the three theories take exception to any of the preceding rules?

3. Do you believe that a person ought always tell the truth? Why or why not?

4. Which theory of ethics seems most faithful to the Bible? Give reasons for your answer.

5. What do you think makes a right act right? Why?

7 | PRINCIPLES: What Is the Christian Standard?

What is the Christian standard of morality?

It will come as no surprise to the alert reader to hear that the answer to that one is by no means unanimous! Significant agreements among Christians are matched by equally significant disagreements. Examples:

Christians agree that God is the center and source of all value and the ultimate judge of right and wrong. They disagree—in many cases—about what God approves or condemns.

Christians agree that man's fundamental moral responsibility is to do what God requires and enables him to do. They disagree about what God wills.

Christians agree that the heart of man's problem is the problem of the heart, so Christian conduct depends on Christian conversion. They disagree about what conversion involves.

Christians agree that man is to love his neighbor. They disagree about what love demands and forbids.

Christians agree that the Bible is authoritative for practice as well as faith. They disagree about the nature of its authority and about its proper use.

In this chapter we are going to focus attention on some of the points at issue among Christians as they seek to clarify for themselves the will of him whom they serve in common allegiance. The disagreements discussed should be examined against the background of shared convictions.

The central conviction shared by all Christians is that God's will is the ultimate criterion of right and wrong. Fundamental differences arise as Christians move to identify the content of that will. There are three basic ways of understanding God's will, and three corresponding ways of expressing the Christian theory of ethics.

Some Christians think of God's will as his purpose, plan, or intention. According to these Christians, an act is right if and only if it serves God's cause or helps to realize God's intention. Advocates of this position are Christian results-ethicists.

Other Christians think of God's will primarily as his law, commandment, or mandate. According to these Christians, an act is right if and only if it conforms to God's law. This, of course, is Christian duty-ethics.

Still other Christians think of God's will as his work, his activity, his deeds in history. Christian responsibility-ethicists hold that an act is right if and only if it is the fitting response to God's activity.

All three ways of thinking about what God requires and enables us to do may be found in the Bible. Christian results-ethicists, for example, can support their way of defining God's will for man by citing such passages as these: ". . . seek first his kingdom and his righteousness . . ." (Matt. 6:33). ". . . he has made known to us . . . the mystery of his will . . . which he set forth in Christ as a plan for the fulness of time, to unite all things in him. . . . we who first hoped in Christ have been destined and appointed to live for the praise of his glory" (Eph. 1:9-12). "You did not choose me, but I chose you and appointed you that you should go and bear fruit and that your fruit should abide . . ." (John 15:16). "Let no one seek his own good, but the good of his neighbor"

(1 Cor. 10:24). ". . . whether you eat or drink, or whatever you do, do all to the glory of God" (1 Cor. 10:31). ". . . be perfect, as your heavenly Father is perfect" (Matt. 5:48).

No one confronted with such goal-oriented passages as these can doubt the biblical basis for thinking of the Christian moral life in terms of ends and ideals. Why are we here? What is the purpose for which we live? What is the ideal we are called to realize? What is the chief end of man?

Christians who ask the moral question in this way often speak of the Christian responsibility as that of "glorifying God" or "bringing in the kingdom" or "realizing the fatherhood of God and the brotherhood of man." They begin with some ideal, some vision of the way things ought to be, some great cause or objective or goal, and they see their responsibility as that of realizing this ideal, fulfilling this vision, achieving this goal. Thus they pray, "Thy kingdom come," and look forward to and work for the time when the kingdoms of this world shall become the kingdom of our Lord Jesus Christ. They hear the Sermon on the Mount as a description of the good and faithful life, and try to shape their existence in light of this ideal. Or they catch a vision of the unity of mankind in Jesus Christ, and try to realize, to make concrete, this vision as they live life with others.

Christian duty-ethicists think of God's will not so much in terms of his intention as in terms of his claim. What is our duty? It is not to realize some future goal. It is to obey the present commandment of God. "He has showed you, O man, what is good; and what does the LORD require of you but to do justice, and to love kindness, and to walk humbly with your God?" (Micah 6:8).

Christians of this tradition have a profound sense of the immediacy and inescapable clarity of God's claim. What does God enable and require us to do? The word has been given: ". . . love the Lord your God with all your heart. . . . love your neighbor as yourself" (Mark 12:30, 31). ". . . be holy, for I am holy" (Lev. 11:44, 45; 1 Peter 1:16). ". . . deny [yourself] and take up [your] cross and follow me" (Mark 8:34). ". . . cease to do evil, learn to do good; seek justice, correct oppression; defend the fatherless, plead for the widow" (Isa. 1:16-17). In whatever way obedience to these commandments may take shape in a particular situation, the ultimate responsibility of the Christian is clear: he is to obey the law of the Lord to whom he belongs. Right action is action which conforms to God's command.

Christian responsibility-ethicists, who think of God's will in terms of his action, and of man's obligation in terms of making fitting response, contend that the biblical ethic is best understood when viewed in this light. Says Niebuhr:

> At the critical junctures in the history of Israel and of the early Christian community the decisive question men raised was not "What is the goal?" nor yet "What is the law?" but "What is happening?" and then "What is the fitting response to what is happening?" When an Isaiah counsels his people, he does not remind them of the law they are required to obey nor yet of the goal toward which they are directed but calls to their attention the intentions of God present in hiddenness in the actions of Israel's enemies. The question he and his peers raise in every critical moment is about the interpretation of what is going on, whether what is happening be, im-

mediately considered, a drought or the invasion of a foreign army, or the fall of a great empire. Israel is the people that is to see and understand the action of God in everything that happens and to make a fitting reply. So it is in the New Testament also. The God to whom Jesus points is not the commander who gives laws but the doer of small and of mighty deeds, the creator of sparrows and clother of lilies, the ultimate giver of blindness and of sight, the ruler whose rule is hidden in the manifold activities of plural agencies but is yet in a way visible to those who know how to interpret the signs of the times.[1]

EXAMPLES: Because Assyria, though it does not know or intend it, is the rod of God's anger in judgment against his people, the first thing Israel ought to do in response to the Assyrian invasion is to repent (Isa. 10:5-19). Because the Lord has anointed Cyrus to deliver his people from their Babylonian captivity, their fitting response to what is going on is to lift up their voice in joy (Isa. 45:1-8; 40:1-11). Because the time is fulfilled and the kingdom of God is at hand, man's appropriate action is to repent and believe the gospel (Mark 1:15). Because God loves his enemies and makes his sun rise on the evil as well as on the good, it is only fitting that man should love his enemies (Matt. 5:44-45). Because the Father is working still, it is only appropriate that the Son works (John 5:17). Because God has so loved us, we ought to love one another (1 John 4:11).

In summary, all Christians agree that the ultimate criterion of right and wrong is the will of God, but they disagree about how best to grasp and express that will. Some think of God's will in terms of his plan, and man's obligation in terms of goal-oriented action. Others identify God's will as his commandment, and man's duty as obedience to law. Still others say that God's will is his activity, and man's responsibility is to make a fitting response.

Let's look now at some examples among contemporary American Christian ethicists of these three ways of thinking of God's will and man's responsibility.

The Christian Life as Service to God's Cause

John C. Bennett proposes that we flesh out the Christian moral standard by clarifying the goals for which we Christians should aim.[2] According to him, we should bring two types of ethical criteria as guidance to every social situation: a set of very broad goals for society and some more specific objectives which belong to a particular historical period.

By broad goals, Bennett means such values as order, freedom, justice, the openness of society to truth, and the need for productivity or concern for the material conditions of welfare. Such general goals emerge from reflection on (1) what love requires, (2) what the good of the neighbor is in the world as we know it (that is, what his needs are in our contemporary situation), and (3) Christian teachings about man, his relationship to God, his social nature, his sin and freedom, and the like.

Goals such as order, freedom, and justice are obviously abstract, each needs careful definition, and they often conflict. Recent debates in our country between advocates of "law and order" on the one hand and supporters of "freedom" or "justice" on the other demonstrate the tensions between these goals. But, according to Bennett, it is precisely because all of them are values for society that we dare not drop any one of them as a vital concern—despite the difficulties we have in relating them. Moreover, we need to do a lot of before-a-crisis-hits thinking about how we believe order and freedom, for example, ought to be arranged in priority. Are there times when it is justifiable to risk the loss of order for the sake of freedom? the loss of freedom for the sake of order? Under what conditions would it be appropriate to subordinate one concern to the other?

These broad criteria should lead us to more specific objectives which belong to a particular historical period. Such objectives should make particular reference to our concrete situation and determine or help to determine policy, but they are not identical with the concrete policy which is the immediate guide to action. Here are some specific objectives which Bennett claims are implied in Christian faith and ethics for our time even though they are by no means exclusively Christian:

> The prevention of general nuclear war.
>
> The working out of moral limits for the conduct of any military operations.
>
> The concern for the maintenance or the development of societies, which are marked by openness and pluralism, in which there are protections of spiritual and cultural freedom.
>
> The acceptance of the responsibility of the nation acting through government to maintain the stability of the economy and to develop the essential conditions of welfare for the whole population.[3]

To summarize, Bennett proposes that we develop content for the Christian standard or guideline for action by moving from our *ultimate norm*—the will of God or

love for the neighbor—to slightly *more specific principles*
—for example, God wills peace and justice; to *specific
objectives* relevant to our time and place in history—for
example, we must prevent general nuclear war; to *public
policies*—for example, we should seek disarmament
agreements with the Soviet Union; to *actions* based on
those policies—for example, we should explore the possibilities of entering a strategic arms limitations treaty.

At each stage, of course, the possibility for error
and self-deception increases; so one can affirm that God
wills peace and justice with a good deal more confidence
than one can affirm that he wills the SALT talks. Nevertheless, this process of goal-clarification enables the
Christian to offer reasons for his reasons and provides
guidance for his decision-making.

Critics charge that this procedure is so abstract as
to be arid and unrealistic. Freedom, order, and justice,
they contend, are not independent realities divorced from
the common life. They are relations among specific men
and groups. What good does it do, for example, to set
"economic justice" as a goal for society, and then develop a hypothetical statement of what a just distribution
of wealth might be? Management and labor could well
agree on the abstract and hypothetical goal—and still
not move one inch forward in contract negotiations! [4]

Bennett would probably respond to such criticism by
acknowledging the danger of our becoming abstract and
unrealistic in our goal-setting. However, he would probably counter by reminding his critics of the values in
clarifying for ourselves general and specific goals. One
value is that it forces us to see what price we have to pay
in terms of one objective when we commit ourselves to
another. If, for example, I am asked to sacrifice peace

Crane.

He doesn't lack for answers
but he doesn't seem to
listen for the questions.

for the sake of justice, I ought to know exactly what is being requested of me. If, on the other hand, I am tempted to buy "peace at any price," I ought to see as clearly as possible just what that price is.

A second value in clarifying goals is that it lessens the danger of single-track devotion to one ethical principle. "Better dead than Red" is a catchy slogan, but is it an adequate ethical principle? Should it be the primary principle shaping foreign policy?

A third value in clarifying goals is that it enables the Christian to approach a concrete decision with a little something more than simply the desire to do the right or loving or fitting thing.

The Christian Life as Obedience to God's Law

The duty-ethics tradition in Christian ethics identifies "doing God's will" with "conforming to God's law." Christians in this tradition tend to agree not only that obedience to God's law is properly the primary ethical concern of the Christian, but also that, as Paul said, "the whole law is fulfilled in one word, 'You shall love your neighbor as yourself' " (Gal. 5:14). They disagree—strongly—as to (1) whether the love commandment is the *only* commandment that is absolutely binding on the Christian at all times and in all places, and (2) what the love commandment requires.

Joseph Fletcher, whose book *Situation Ethics* was a best seller and the center of a storm of controversy when it came out in 1966, contends that love is the only norm for the Christian, the only thing that is always good. Says Fletcher:

> [Love] is a principle, a "formal" principle, expressing what type of real actions Christians are to call good. . . . It is the *only* principle that always obliges us in conscience. Unlike all other principles you might mention, love alone when well served is always good and right in every situation.[5]

> . . . *Christian* situation ethics has only one norm or principle or law (call it what you will) that is binding and unexceptionable, always good and right regardless of the circumstances. That is "love"—the *agapē* of the summary commandment to love God and the neighbor. Everything else without exception, all laws and rules and principles and ideals and norms, are only *contingent,* only valid *if they happen* to serve love in any situation.[6]

Fletcher is not quite as radical as he sounds. For example, having thrown all other norms or principles or laws (call them what you will) out the front door, Fletcher lets in through the back door utilitarianism (a results-ethics theory which asserts that we ought always to seek the greatest good of the greatest number):

> Justice is love coping with situations where distribution is called for. On this basis it becomes plain that as the love ethic searches seriously for a social policy it must form a coalition with utilitarianism. It takes over from Bentham and Mill the strategic principle of "the greatest good of the greatest number."
>
> Observe that this is a genuine coalition, even though it reshapes the "good" of the utilitarians, replacing their pleasure principle with *agapē*. In the coalition the [goal] . . . becomes . . . the greatest amount of neighbor welfare for the largest number of neighbors possible.[7]

God's will has now been defined not only as "love your neighbor" but also as "seek the greatest amount of neighbor welfare for the largest number of neighbors possible." Moreover, in his discussion of an abortion case, Fletcher seems to proclaim yet another norm or principle or law that is always binding and unexceptionable regardless of the circumstances, namely, *"no unwanted and unintended* baby should ever be born."[8] However, despite these and other apparent inconsistencies in his position, Fletcher repeatedly claims that love and love alone is an absolute norm for the Christian.

At the other end of the duty-ethics spectrum, Carl F. H. Henry, voicing a conservative or evangelical posi-

tion, argues vigorously that God in his mercy has given
us considerable more guidance for the Christian life than
the single commandment of love. Says Henry:

> Love, as the Bible exposits it, is not something
> as nebulous as moderns would have us think. The
> New Testament knows nothing of lawless believers
> in Christ. No believer is left to work out his moral
> solutions by the principle of love alone. He has some
> external guidance from Divine revelation. The early
> believers were not delivered from an obligation to
> obey the precepts of the law. The life of love which
> Christianity proclaims is centered in love for the
> Living God who has revealed his will, and only to
> the extent that love impels the believer to fulfill
> God's revealed will is it genuinely of the Holy
> Spirit. Love is in accord with the biblical ethic
> when it devotedly seeks to obey fully the Divine
> commands.
>
> The content of love must be defined by Divine
> revelation. The biblical revelation places the only
> reliable rule of practice before the community of
> faith. What the Bible teaches gives trustworthy di-
> rection to love of self, of neighbor, of God.[9]

How do you find content for the command to love?
By turning to the Bible, says Henry. The Ten Commandments express fundamental norms which are binding on Christians in both their religious and ethical dimensions. The prophets reveal the deep meaning of these
commandments. The Sermon on the Mount makes clear
not only the disposition God desires, but also additional precepts and commandments. Because the Bible
sets forth so clearly what it means to fulfill the love of

God, Henry claims, there is no reason any man "need be in doubt about what inner attitudes and pursuits are approved by God, and what are condemned." [10]

Many contemporary Christians who share Henry's conviction that "what the Bible teaches gives trustworthy direction to love" lack his confidence that it leaves no doubt about what action is divinely approved or condemned. Why? Because of questions like these: How do you determine which biblical commandments are really God's? How do you interpret the commandments accepted as authoritative? How do you handle conflicts between two apparently authoritative commandments? How do you "apply" the most binding commandment to the situation at hand? Puzzled by these questions, such Christians take some small measure of comfort upon discovering that even Henry recognizes that however infallible the Word may be, the man who interprets it is fallible:

> . . . even consecrated Christians, devoted to the will of God, and seeking the guidance of the Holy Spirit in applying the ethics of inspiration in their immediate situation, have had to confess at times that some other biblical principle should have been applied, or that a mistake was sincerely made.[11]

Paul Ramsey is a contemporary Christian duty-ethicist who avoids the legalism of Henry on the right and yet sees much more content in the Christian norm of love than does Fletcher on the left. When he published his *Basic Christian Ethics* in 1950, Ramsey's primary target for criticism was legalism in Christian morality. Quoting with approval Emil Brunner's observation that ". . . There is obviously a great deal written in the Old

Testament as divine law which no Christian can regard
as binding upon himself unless he ceases to be a Christian," [12] Ramsey went on to argue that everything is
lawful, everything is permitted, which Christian love permits. The Christian ethic is an ethic without rules. What
should be done or not be done in a particular instance,
what is good or bad, right or wrong, cannot be known
in advance or derived from some preconceived code. What
is required is derived *backward* by Christian love from
what it understands to be the needs of others.

On principle, then, the Christian ethic is more
lenient, that is, freer from regulation, than any other. At
the same time, it is severer with itself, more subject to
command; for while everything is permitted which Christian love permits, everything is demanded which Christian love requires. Thus the liberty of the Christian man
is matched with his slavery to Christ. Freedom from the
law belongs only to that person who is free for reason
of the most terrifying obligation. "The commands of
love are as stringent as the needs of the world are
urgent. . . ." [13]

In more recent years, Ramsey has been less concerned with the legalism of conservative Christians than
with the relativism of Christian situationists, on the one
hand, and the utilitarianism of Christian goal-setters, on
the other. In arguments with both, his starting point remains love as the ultimate norm for the Christian. We are
always permitted to do what love permits, required to do
what love demands, prohibited from doing what love
forbids.

Against situationists, who contend that love alone is
always binding, Ramsey argues that there are some general rules or principles or virtues or styles of life which

always embody love and therefore are always incumbent on the Christian. The characteristics of love set forth in 1 Corinthians 13, for example, are universal statements of what love requires.

Against results-ethicists, who contend that the right is determined by results, Ramsey argues that *"How* we do *what* we do is as important as our goals."[14] Ramsey's basic position is this: ". . . love posits or takes form in principles of right conduct which express the difference it discerns between permitted and prohibited action, and these are not wholly derived from reflection upon the consequences."[15] He seeks to provide content for the Christian standard by exploring and clarifying these principles, rules, and practices of conduct which love prohibits or requires.

The Christian Life as Response to God's Activity

Christian results-ethicists maintain that God calls us to work for his goals. These people provide content for the Christian standard by indicating what those goals are. Christian duty-ethicists assert that God demands that we conform to his laws. They elaborate the standard by clarifying those laws. Christian responsibility-ethicists contend that God requires response to his action. To them belongs the awesome job of interpreting what God is doing.

Paul Lehmann is an influential American ethicist in this third tradition. In a widely read essay published in 1953, Lehmann wrote:

> . . . an ethic, based upon the self-revelation of God in Jesus Christ, is more concerned about "The Divine Indicative" than it is about the "Divine Im-

perative." The primary question is not, "What does God command?" The primary question is "What does God do?" [16]

Lehmann answers his own question in various ways in that essay. God acts characteristically in a historical way. He wills to include men in fellowship with himself and to establish the conditions under which men can really be themselves in being related to each other. He offers his love to men in faithfulness and trust, to be faithfully and trustfully received. He brings in his kingdom. He establishes his *koinonia* (community or fellowship; namely, the church) as the outpost of his judgment upon every social pattern or structure which seeks to preserve and to justify itself by the idolatry of the status quo, and as the place for renewal and establishment of new patterns and structures.

There are many ways to describe God's activities. However, the three key words which best describe God's concrete action in the world are forgiveness, justice, and reconciliation. These words also describe the pattern and direction of the Christian life which is lived in response to divine action. Christian behavior moves along a line which may be plotted graphically by three points. The first point is forgiveness, which is the gift, free and undeserved, of a new possibility of life. At the other end of the line is reconciliation, the actual condition which emerges whenever the alienation of enmity has been transmitted into fellowship. In between —not in the middle, but somewhere along the line, on the concrete way from forgiveness to reconciliation—is what the Bible calls "justice." Writes Lehmann:

Justice is God's setting right what is not right in the

doing of His will in the world. This happens—as it looks from within the *koinonia*—whenever existing cultural and social patterns, existing structures of power and pretension, whether corporate or private, are broken down and overthrown, while others are built and planted.[17]

Lehmann uses other terminology to describe God's activity in his book *Ethics in a Christian Context,* published in 1963. There he describes God's activity as "political" activity, using the term as the Greek philosopher Aristotle used it, meaning "to make and keep human life *human* in the world." Thus Lehmann writes:

What God is doing in the world is setting up and carrying out the conditions for what it takes to keep human life human. The fruit of this divine activity is human maturity, the wholeness of every man and of all men in the new humanity inaugurated and being fulfilled by Jesus Christ in the world.[18]

Harvey Cox is another Christian ethicist who sees the Christian life as one of response to God's activity. In his theological best seller *The Secular City,* he popularized Archie Hargraves' graphic analogy: God's work in the world is like a floating crap game, and the church is a confirmed gambler whose "major compulsion upon arising each day is to know where the action is" so he can run there and "dig it." [19] According to Cox, the keys to locating "where the action is" are the Exodus and Easter. Says Cox:

The Exodus is the event which sets forth "what God is doing in history." He is seen to be liberating people from bondage, releasing them from political,

cultural, and economic captivity, providing them
with the occasion to forge in the wilderness a new
symbol system, a new set of values, and a new national identity. Easter means that the same activity
goes on today, and that where such liberating activity occurs, the same Yahweh of Hosts is at work.
Both Exodus and Easter are caught up in the inclusive symbol of the Kingdom, the realization of
the liberating rule of God.[20]

H. Richard Niebuhr offers a considerably more complex statement of God's activity than either Lehmann or
Cox. The God whom he believes is acting in all actions
upon us is the trinitarian God who is always and in every
action Creator, Governor, and Redeemer. As Creator,
he manifests himself as power; as Governor and Judge,
he manifests himself as order; as Redeemer, he manifests
himself as goodness and mercy. The appropriate response
to his creative activity in everything that happens is affirmation, the search for understanding, the cultivation of
what he has made, and man's own creativity. The fitting
response to his governing activity is the acceptance of
one's limitations, repentance, self-denial, and the restraint
of others. The fitting response to God's redemptive activity is trust, freedom, forgiveness, gratitude, joy.[21]

Of the three principal ways of describing the moral
life of a Christian, I find the ethics of responsibility most
helpful for two basic reasons:

1. I believe that the understanding of man as moral
agent, on which it is based, is accurate. That understanding, as we saw in the last chapter, is that man in his moral
life is man the answerer, the responder to action upon
him or around him as he interprets that action. The

theory assumes that in every moral judgment what I declare to be right is what I believe to be fitting, and that I believe it is right because I believe it is fitting.

As I reflect on my own judgment-making processes, I find this to be the case. I certainly consider both causes and principles as I make decisions. I keep in mind both goals and laws. But even as I do this, I finally conclude that a particular act is right because it is *fitting*—fitting, in part, because of my goals or principles, but fitting also because, everything considered, this is simply what I ought to do. Moreover, when I consider the moral judgments and actions of my companions, it appears to me that they also do those things which seem fitting to them in light of their perceptions, presuppositions, principles, primary concerns.

Now, if in fact every man's sense of obligation is the feeling that he ought to do the fitting thing in the situation in which he finds himself, as this theory assumes, then it is critically important for us to clarify for ourselves as well as possible just what that situation is—which this theory does. The Christian ethic of responsibility defines my situation as that of one who is confronted by God in every event. As Niebuhr puts it: "Responsibility affirms: 'God is acting in all actions upon you. So respond to all actions upon you as to respond to his action.' " [22]

2. I find this way of thinking about man in his life before God a helpful key to understanding the biblical ethic. The Bible clearly deals with goals and intentions, and even more explicitly with laws and commandments. But once you think of the Bible as a witness to God's action and his call to man to make suitable response, traces of this responsibility motif can be found practically everywhere.

No type of Christian ethics is without its peculiar difficulties. Christian results-ethicists continually have to fight against abstractness. Sure, everyone is for peace and order and freedom and justice, but what concretely is the meaning of these relationships among men? Christian duty-ethicists continually have to resist temptations to legalism and self-righteousness. Principles can become more important than people, correct behavior more important than compassionate concern. The peculiar difficulty of the responsibility-ethicist lies in interpreting what God is doing. Joseph Fletcher flatly denies that any man can know what God is up to:

> It is tricky enough to decide what course is the most loving one, but I can do it with more or less assurance. However, to assert in a civil war, for example, or a strike, or in any complex "gray area," that God is on this or that side is plainly demonic, idolatrous, or psychotic. My faith in God is not some kind of tracer ink with which I can splatter God, so that I may find him when I look for him in spite of my humanly limited perception of God's own [concealment]. Love I can do, but God's will I can do only through love.[23]

Why Fletcher feels greater self-confidence in being able to identify "the most loving course" than he does in being able to identify "the most responsive-to-God action" is not at all clear to me. The problem seems equally tricky in either case. Be that as it may, Fletcher is surely right in questioning the claim of any Christian who reports that he knows what God is up to in any complex situation. The warning of Jesus, though spoken to a different issue, certainly hangs heavy-heavy over any such

Christian's head: ". . . if any one says to you, 'Lo, here is the Christ!' or 'There he is!' do not believe it" (Matt. 24:23).

The fact that we cannot know everything we would like to know about God's action and our responsibility, however, does not mean that we are completely without understanding. In the final chapter I indicate how I think we can most responsibly seek to discern what God enables and requires us to do.

QUESTIONS FOR THOUGHT AND DISCUSSION

1. What are the strengths and weaknesses of each of the three types of Christian ethics?

2. Which type do you find most helpful? Why? How do you guard against its built-in dangers?

3. Select one of the three examples with which chapter 5 ended, and indicate the answer and justification for his answer that might be given by a Christian (*a*) results-ethicist, (*b*) duty-ethicist, and (*c*) responsibility-ethicist.

8 | PROCEDURE: Some Things to Keep in Mind

Dear Son,

Thanks for your good letter. Your mother and I knew that we would miss you when you went off to college, but I'm afraid we didn't realize quite how much we would miss having you around the house. It's good to know that you miss us too. It's even better to hear that you find college life stimulating, demanding, upsetting, and exciting.

This letter is my response to your rather remarkable request that I put down on paper everything that I think a Christian ought to keep in mind as he makes a moral judgment about a really critical issue, such as whether he should apply for conscientious objector status. That's a tall order! My answer, I'm afraid, is a long letter. Just remember that you asked for it!

I want to preface what follows with this observation: Moral judgment-making is a much more dynamic process than a listing of "everything one ought to keep in mind" would imply. Keeping certain things in mind, and thinking them through, are surely important in decision-making. But so are upbringing, character, maturity, emotions, imagination—and "gut reactions." The whole man, not just his mind, makes the decision. I think we can understand many of the factors that enter into our judgments. And I think we ought to be prepared to defend the decisions we make. But who can ever fully understand what, in the final analysis, led him to conclude that he ought to do one thing rather than another? The moral life—like every other significant human activity—is filled with mystery.

In my customary sermonic way, I've organized my thoughts around four main points. (You can take the preacher out of the pulpit, but . . .) I've even looked up some biblical passages and a few other quotations for you to think about. But I hope I don't sound hopelessly preachy to you. And please don't interpret what follows as an artificial, wooden scheme or checklist of twenty things that you must absolutely consider before you can finally make up your mind. Play it loose.

I think a Christian makes a moral judgment most responsibly when he makes it with the commitment of *faith*, in light of the *facts*, with the help of the *fellowship*, and aware of his own *fallibility*. Here, then, are my proposals:

A. *Make your judgment with the commitment of faith.* That's shorthand for "the commitment of faith in the God and Father of our Lord Jesus Christ." You and I and everyone else inevitably make our judgments with the commitment of faith in *some* object of devotion— whether it be the self, the family, the nation, humanity, or some other great value. Our problem, therefore, is not to "whomp up" some trust and loyalty but to direct our devotion to the only one who is ultimately worthy of it. (I think Jesus is our Savior precisely because he enables us to do that. But that's another story.) But what does it mean to make your judgment with the commitment of faith in God? I have eight suggestions. (Eight?! Have mercy, Dad.)

1. Make your judgment with the *self-understanding* that comes with faith. Remember who you are and whose you are. Remember that your father was a "wandering

Aramean" whom the Lord liberated from Egypt (Deut. 26:5-10). Remember that once you were nobody, but now you are somebody (1 Peter 2:10). Remember that while you were yet helpless, Christ died for you (Rom. 5:6-8). Remember that you are not your own; you were bought with a price (1 Cor. 6:19-20). Remember that you did not receive the spirit of slavery; you received the spirit of sonship (Rom. 8:15). Remember that you are a child of God, and that you belong, heart, soul, mind, and strength, to him. Remember that you are ultimately accountable to him to whom you belong. God—not your friends, your folks, your church, your nation, or anyone else, but God—is the final one to whom you must answer for your decision.

2. Make your judgment with the *motive* that accompanies faith. That motive, I believe, is with awe-filled gratitude, or grateful awe. So be grateful for grace, and show your gratitude. Have mercy, because God is merciful to you. Forgive, because you live in forgiveness. Seek justice, because God's judgment is just. Love, because God first loved you. Remember Paul's plea: "I appeal to you, therefore, brethren, by the mercies of God . . ." (Rom. 12:1). Old John Calvin was right: "Ever since God exhibited himself to us as a Father, we must be convicted of extreme ingratitude if we do not in turn exhibit ourselves as his sons." [1]

Powerful though gratitude is as a motive, however, you need not depend on this feeling alone to move you to responsible action. When we are at our best, perhaps, we say to God, "Your wish is my command." But often we are not at our best. Don't bank too heavily on a feeling of thankfulness. Don't become sentimental. Remember that the Lord our God is holy. It was not merely gratitude which moved Moses to exchange the easy life of Midian for the blood, sweat, and tears of Egypt; it was also healthy respect for the Lord's ability to do remarkable things with fire (Exod. 3:1—4:17). It was not simply a feeling of thankfulness which prompted Isaiah to volunteer for prophetic duty; it was also all that smoke that filled the temple (Isa. 6:1-8). It was not solely a cheery desire to please that sent Amos to Bethel; it was also hearing that lion roar (Amos 7:14-15, 3:8). In Gethsemane, Jesus' sweat became like "great drops of blood falling down upon the ground" (Luke 22:44). When gratitude runs low, remember that "it is a fearful thing to fall into the hands of the living God" (Heb. 10:31).

3. Make your judgment in the *confidence* of faith. Trust that God is already at work for good in the situation you face, no matter how dismal that situation appears to you (Rom. 8:28). Our friends in the Movement (as well as lots of other folk!) are not the only ones concerned for peace and freedom and justice. God is also concerned. And he is doing something about it. Moses believed this. That's another reason he went back to Egypt: the one who called him to work for the liberation of his people had seen their affliction and heard their cry, and *he* was going to deliver them (Exod. 3:7-9). God simply asked Moses to help! Jesus put it this way: "My Father is working still, and I am working" (John 5:17). Remember, then, that there is nothing over which God doesn't rule, nothing in which he is not involved. That means that even in tragedy, waste, and human destructiveness there is still a goodness that can be realized, a possibility of renewal.

4. Make your judgment with the *inquiry* of faith. Ask: What does *God* require and enable me to do here

and now? You can ask this question in at least three ways: What is God's *purpose* here that I am to serve? Or, What is God's *law* here that I am to obey? Or, What is God's *action* here to which I should make fitting response? You need not choose one way of asking the question to the exclusion of the other two. Reflection on God's purposes and commandments gives insight into his action, and vice versa.

For me the most helpful way of raising the inquiry of faith is to ask, What is the God whom I have met in Jesus Christ doing in this situation as Creator, Governor, and Redeemer? What is his work for good in this time and place and set of circumstances? And then, what am I to do in response to divine action? What ought to and can be done here and now which, at least in some fragmentary way, will be a response both to the divine sustenance, judgment, and redemption and to the concrete needs before me? Clyde A. Holbrook once described the man I would like to be with these words:

> . . . a man of faith, in gratitude, puts himself responsibly and sensitively at the disposal of God's will for a situation, to the limits of his reason, imagination, and courage. He does not presume to read off in advance what God wills in detail, nor does he assume that he will be miraculously safeguarded from errors of discrimination. He does not cast into an artificial wooden scheme the ambiguous particulars of a morally problematic situation. But he does hold himself alert and responsive to what God lays upon him through his neighbor's need.[2]

5. Make your judgment with the *intentions* of faith. Your moral action is governed in part by your intentions

—that is, by your thought about the purposes you are seeking to fulfill, the ends you are seeking to achieve. Your intentions, in turn, are shaped by what you value, what you believe to be worthy of achieving, what you hold to be obligatory, what you have given your loyalty to. To decide in loyalty to Jesus Christ is to decide with intentions that are consistent with such loyalty, and from inferences drawn from what is known in and through him.[3]

Paul proposes a basic intention for all Christians when he says, "whatever you do, do all to the glory of God" (1 Cor. 10:31). This fundamental (and not exclusively moral) intention can function as a touchstone for various moral intentions. You can ask, for example: What moral intentions would not glorify God? What would be contrary to what I believe God to be, will, and do? What moral intentions would glorify God? What would be consistent with the beliefs that are characteristic of faith in him?

In the same passage in which Paul proposes this fundamental intention (1 Cor. 10:23—11:1), he suggests some other intentions that seem proper for Christians. We are not to seek our own good, but the neighbor's. We are to do what is helpful, what builds up. We are to imitate Christ. We are to preserve the liberty of our own conscience. We are to consider the conscience of others.

Such intentions illumine options that are before us. They are not in themselves sufficient to determine what we ought to do in specific situations. Even if you intend to seek the neighbor's good, you do not automatically know what deed will achieve that good for him. Facts must be joined with faith. But your intention can become one of the rules or principles or guidelines involved in your specific judgment. You can ask yourself: What does the central intention to seek the neighbor's good require in this time and place?

6. Make your judgment using the *standard* of faith. Take seriously the rules, principles, guidelines, ways of understanding God's activity and purposes, and the like which are given to us in the Bible. The Bible is the written testimony to and instrument of God's revelation of himself. It witnesses to "the mighty acts of God" in the past, and thereby provides irreplaceable clues for understanding his present activity. It records the response God called for from our forefathers in the faith, and therein offers analogies for our proper response today. The Bible also speaks of the dispositions, intentions, motives, concerns, and deeds appropriate for the man of faith. It reports what many regard as the central moral norm for the Christian: ". . . love one another as I have loved you" (John 15:12). In whatever way you raise the inquiry of faith—whether you ask primarily about God's activity, God's purpose, or God's laws—you will need, if you are asking the question seriously, to be well versed in the witness of Holy Writ. So study your Bible.

Remember as you study it, however, that the simple teachings of Jesus, for example, are not nearly so simple as we are certain to hope for and likely to assume. Biblical scholars as well as we ordinary folk understand them in amazingly different ways. So don't just read the Bible —*study* it. And recognize that we don't "get the word" every time we study the Word.

7. Make your judgment in the *freedom* of faith. God loves you not because you are good, but because *he* is good. You don't have to earn his approval. He has already accepted you. To be sure, he loves you so much

that he is not going to let you alone. God continually disturbs, prods, judges, and overrules us, and when we make wrong judgments, we—and probably others— eventually suffer for them. What doesn't fit in with what the Lord of history is doing eventually gets corrected and changed. So take your judgment-making seriously. But not too seriously. Don't freeze up for fear of making a mistake. Your life in the eyes of God—the only one whose judgment really counts—doesn't depend on your being right!

8. Finally, make your judgment with the *prayer* of faith. Ask God to help you decide what to do. You are not likely to hear any mysterious voice giving a precise answer. But if you open yourself to the Lord, earnestly asking for his guidance, you are likely to receive some clearer sense of what you ought to do. And if the decision is really critical, you need all the help you can get!

So much for what I mean by "make your judgment with the commitment of faith." My other three points— I promise you—aren't nearly as long as this one.

B. *Make your judgment in light of the facts.* "A valid Christian decision," Alexander Miller once wrote, "is compound always of both *faith* and *facts*. It is likely to be valid in the degree to which the faith is rightly apprehended and the facts are rightly measured." [4] Implications:

1. Get the facts. Avoid—like the plague—rumors, lies, gossip, hearsay, ignorance, misunderstandings. Don't trust anyone over thirty. Don't trust anyone under thirty either. Read press releases with skepticism. Look for the whitewash in White Papers. Take everything you are told (including all my advice) with a grain of salt. Find out

as much as you can for yourself. Depend as little as possible on the reports of others.

2. Get as many of the facts as you possibly can. You'll never get "the truth, the whole truth, and nothing but the truth"—but let this be your goal. Be aware of your own bias and blind spots. Remember everything you'll learn in psychology courses about "selective perception" and all you'll read in sociology about social conditioning. Get as many different readings of the situation at hand as possible. Check your version of the facts against those of others.

3. Clarify issues carefully, weigh options deliberately, and recognize—with pain—what values you will have to deny in the very act of affirming others. I would hate for you to wander around in a zombie-like state of numbness and indecision simply because you recognize the complexity of moral dilemmas. I would be just as disappointed if you had nothing of the "tragic sense of life." As you struggle with critical decisions, take comfort in the fact that Jesus sweat blood in the garden.

4. Have a heart, but use your head. Read statistics of human misery with compassion. Put yourself in the other guy's place. Use your imagination. Listen for the sounds of silence. But use your head also. "Make love not war" is as superficial a slogan as is "Better dead than Red." Don't become sentimental, flabby, vague. As you read statistics with compassion, work for remedies that are pragmatic. Be tough-minded. There is no substitute for factual knowledge and conceptional clarity. The gospel that we are saved by grace, not knowledge, is no excuse for acquiescing in ignorance.

C. *Make your judgment with the help of the fellowship.* The church is by no means always right, consistent, or unanimous; even if it were, I would not want you to shift the burden of your decision-making responsibility to it. Still, two heads are often better than one; so pick the brains of the church. This means:

1. Claim your inheritance as a member of a company that's been in business two thousand years since Christ's time—and that doesn't even count the two thousand years the community struggled with moral problems before Christ came! The church has a great moral tradition, a body of moral rules, principles, doctrines, and other teachings which is yours for the asking.

Your generation, for example, is not the first to wonder about the conditions under which a conscientious man can go to war. Christians have worried about that one since New Testament days, and a widely accepted doctrine of the "just war" emerged in the fourth century only to be worked on and refined ever since. Our troubled age is not the first to wonder what in the world God is up to when nations and empires rise and fall. Augustine's *City of God* deals with precisely that problem. Christians have wanted to know what to make of their sexuality as long as there have been Christians, and lots of answers— good, bad, and indifferent—have been given to the inquiry.

All of these teachings, rules, admonitions, and exhortations are part of the Christian tradition, which helps shape the Christian style of life, of which the Christian standard is a loosely organized verbalization. You certainly don't have to do everything your forefathers said you ought. Following some of their rules would clearly be wrong! But don't ignore the wisdom of the tradition. Claim your inheritance.

2. Read what some contemporary Christian theolo-

gians and ethicists are saying. Study the Niebuhrs, John Bennett, James Gustafson, Paul Lehmann, Paul Ramsey, James Sellers, Roger Shinn, Richard Shaull, and Harvey Cox—just to mention some American Protestant ethicists. Some exciting stuff is being written these days. Don't miss it.

3. Test your tentative conclusions with others in the church, particularly those most likely to disagree with you. Congregations in America are so racially segregated and socioeconomically stratified that one is not likely to have his pet prejudices seriously challenged in the local adult class. You know that. But the same problem exists with the local campus Christian fellowship. And of course in the ecclesiastical bureaucracy. That's why we so need each other. The local congregation, which tends to be conservative, needs to be challenged by the national bureaucracy, which tends to be more liberal; the bureaucracy, in turn, needs to be challenged by the parish to justify its ways; a regional church needs to hear the word of the ecumenical church; and so forth. "To each is given the manifestation of the Spirit for the common

I was confused
about moral judgment.

So I wrote
my dad for help

and waited.

good" (1 Cor. 12:7). Let no man say to another, "I have no need of you." Test your moral judgment in the market-place of the wider fellowship.

D. Finally, *make your judgment in the awareness that you*—like every other man, woman, and child on God's green earth—*are finite, fallible, and amazingly gifted in the fine art of self-deception.*

In any particular decision you may well be mis-taken. No matter how diligently you seek to discern God's activity, how thoroughly you gather factual data, how carefully you weigh various options, or how openly you listen to the counsel of the church—in any given judg-ment, you may well be dead wrong.

So? So do the best you can. In light of all valid considerations, decide what *you* think God requires and enables you to do. Then cast yourself on his forbearance and forgiveness.

That's what it means to decide, act, and live by faith.

Love,
Dad

It came.

With so much to think about I wonder how Jesus ever got anything done.

QUESTIONS FOR THOUGHT AND DISCUSSION

1. What is your overall response to this guideline for making responsible moral judgments? What are its strengths? its weaknesses? Are there any critical omissions?

2. Review what is said about the Christian's motive. Is an act done out of fear of the Lord less valuable than one done out of gratitude for grace? Justify your answer.

3. Study 1 Corinthians 10:23—11:1 in light of the author's comments on intentions. What are some specified intentions for Christians today in the area of world peace that are consistent with the intentions listed by Paul?

NOTES

Chapter 1. What Is a Moral Judgment?

1. Quoted in Joseph Fletcher, *Situation Ethics: The New Morality* (Philadelphia: The Westminster Press, 1966), p. 54.

Chapter 2. How to Analyze Moral Judgments

1. Jeffrey K. Hadden, *The Gathering Storm in the Churches* (Garden City, N.Y.: Doubleday & Co., 1969), *passim*.
2. Waldo Beach, *The Christian Life* (Richmond: The CLC Press, 1966), p. 39.

Chapter 3. Persons: In Whom Do You Trust?

1. H. Richard Niebuhr, "Evangelical and Protestant Ethics," in *The Heritage of the Reformation,* ed. E. J. F. Arndt (New York: Richard R. Smith, 1950), p. 223.
2. This is a way of phrasing the question which I have borrowed, with slight modification, from James M. Gustafson, *Christ and the Moral Life* (New York: Harper & Row, 1968), p. 240. Putting the question this way indicates that a Christian's faith in God can and sometimes does make a significant difference in his moral life; yet, at the same time, no undue claims are made.
3. H. Richard Niebuhr, "The Hidden Church and the Churches in Sight," *Religion in Life,* Vol. XV (1945-46), p. 106.
4. John Calvin, *Institutes of the Christian Religion,* tr. Henry Beveridge (2 vols.; Grand Rapids: Wm. B. Eerdmans Publishing Co., 1957), Bk. III, chap. vii, par. 1.

Chapter 4. Perceptions: What Do You See?

1. Harris Survey, *Richmond News Leader,* September 3, 1969, p. 13.
2. *Ibid.,* September 9, 1969, p. 3.
3. Hadden, *The Gathering Storm in the Churches,* p. 136.
4. Peter L. Berger, *Invitation to Sociology: A Humanistic Perspective* (Garden City, N.Y.: Doubleday Anchor Books, 1963), pp. 80-81.
5. *Ibid.,* p. 120.

6. James M. Gustafson, "Love Monism," in *Storm over Ethics,* by John C. Bennett *et al.* (Philadelphia: United Church Press and the Bethany Press, 1967), p. 32.
7. Frank C. Sharp, *Ethics* (New York: The Century Co., 1928), Chapter VIII.
8. Reinhold Niebuhr, *The Nature and Destiny of Man* (New York: Charles Scribner's Sons, 1949), Vol. II, p. 122.

Chapter 5. Principles: How Do You Tell Right from Wrong?

1. Lyndon B. Johnson, "American Policy in Viet-Nam," Remarks at Johns Hopkins University, April 7, 1965, in *The Viet-Nam Reader: Articles and Documents on American Foreign Policy and the Viet-Nam Crisis,* ed. Marcus G. Raskin and Bernard B. Fall (New York: Random House Vintage Books, 1965), p. 345.
2. Peter L. Berger, "A Conservative Reflection About Vietnam," *Christianity and Crisis,* Vol. XXVII, No. 3 (March 6, 1967), p. 34.
3. Paul Ramsey, "Is Vietnam a Just War?" in his collection of essays *The Just War: Force and Political Responsibility* (New York: Charles Scribner's Sons, 1968), pp. 502-503.
4. Frederick S. Carney, "Deciding in the Situation: What Is Required?" in *Norm and Context in Christian Ethics,* ed. Gene H. Outka and Paul Ramsey (New York: Charles Scribner's Sons, 1968), p. 13.

Chapter 6. Principles: What Makes an Act Right?

1. H. Richard Niebuhr discusses the three types of ethics and the symbols of man they assume in *The Responsible Self: An Essay in Christian Moral Philosophy* (New York: Harper & Row, 1963), chapter 1.
2. William K. Frankena, *Ethics* (Englewood Cliffs, N.J.: Prentice-Hall, 1963), p. 13.

Chapter 7. Principles: What Is the Christian Standard?

1. H. Richard Niebuhr, *The Responsible Self,* p. 67.
2. John C. Bennett, "Principles and the Context," in *Storm over Ethics,* p. 18.
3. *Ibid.*
4. See, for example, James M. Gustafson, "Christian Ethics and Social Policy," in *Faith and Ethics: The Theology of H. Richard Niebuhr,* ed. Paul Ramsey (New York: Harper & Brothers, 1957), pp. 129-130.

5. Fletcher, *Situation Ethics,* p. 60.
6. *Ibid.,* p. 30.
7. *Ibid.,* p. 95.
8. *Ibid.,* p. 39.
9. Carl F. H. Henry, *Christian Personal Ethics* (Grand Rapids: Wm. B. Eerdmans Publishing Co., 1957), p. 255.
10. *Ibid.,* p. 334.
11. *Ibid.,* p. 348.
12. Emil Brunner, *Justice and the Social Order* (New York: Harper & Brothers, 1945), quoted in Paul Ramsey, *Basic Christian Ethics* (New York: Charles Scribner's Sons, 1950), p. 76.
13. Ramsey, *Basic Christian Ethics,* p. 90.
14. Paul Ramsey, *War and the Christian Conscience: How Shall Modern War Be Conducted Justly?* (Durham: Duke University Press, 1961), p. 6.
15. *Ibid.,* p. 4.
16. Paul L. Lehmann, "The Foundation and Pattern of Christian Behavior," in *Christian Faith and Social Action,* ed. John A. Hutchison (New York: Charles Scribner's Sons, 1953), p. 100.
17. *Ibid.,* p. 113.
18. Paul L. Lehmann, *Ethics in a Christian Context* (New York: Harper & Row, 1963), p. 124.
19. Archie Hargraves, "Go Where the Action Is," *Social Action* (February 1964), quoted in Harvey Cox, *The Secular City* (New York: The Macmillan Co., 1965), pp. 125-126.
20. Cox, *The Secular City,* p. 132.
21. James M. Gustafson provides a helpful summary of Niebuhr's theological themes in his Introduction to *The Responsible Self.*
22. H. Richard Niebuhr, *The Responsible Self,* p. 126.
23. Joseph Fletcher, "Reflection and Reply," in *The Situation Ethics Debate,* ed. Harvey Cox (Philadelphia: The Westminster Press, 1968), p. 254.

Chapter 8. Procedure: Some Things to Keep in Mind

1. Calvin, *Institutes,* Bk. III, chap. vi, par. 3.
2. Clyde A. Holbrook, *Faith and Community: A Christian Existential Approach* (New York: Harper & Brothers, 1959), pp. 103-104.
3. See Gustafson, *Christ and the Moral Life,* pp. 256 ff.
4. Alexander Miller, *The Renewal of Man* (Garden City, N.Y.: Doubleday & Co., 1955), p. 94.

SOME HELPFUL BOOKS

Here are the books and essays which most influenced the writing of this book. In each category I have listed works in the order in which I recommend that you read them.

A. General Introductions to Ethics

William K. Frankena, *Ethics* (Englewood Cliffs, N.J.: Prentice-Hall, 1963), a brief (109 pages) and relatively easy introduction for students and the general reader to the branch of philosophy called "ethics."

Richard B. Brandt, *Ethical Theory: The Problems of Normative and Critical Ethics* (Englewood Cliffs, N.J.: Prentice-Hall, 1959), a well-written and widely used college textbook in the field. Not so brief (538 pages).

B. The Nature of Moral Judgments and Judgment-Making

James M. Gustafson, "Moral Discernment in the Christian Life," a twenty-page essay in *Norm and Context in Christian Ethics,* ed. Gene H. Outka and Paul Ramsey (New York: Charles Scribner's Sons, 1968), in which the components in moral judgments are identified.

Frederick S. Carney, "Deciding in the Situation: What Is Required?" a fourteen-page essay in Outka and Ramsey, *Norm and Context,* in which our use of moral rules is explored.

C. Christian Ethics

H. Richard Niebuhr, *The Responsible Self* (New

York: Harper & Row, 1963), in which the three main theories of Christian ethics are discussed, and Jesus' teachings and actions are interpreted in light of responsibility ethics. A difficult but rewarding book.

James M. Gustafson, *Christ and the Moral Life* (New York: Harper & Row, 1968), especially Chapter VII, "Christ and the Moral Life: A Constructive Statement," in which faith's impact on the Christian and his judgments is examined.

Eric Mount, Jr., *Conscience and Responsibility* (Richmond: John Knox Press, 1969), in which man's social existence, the meaning of conscience, and the nature of responsibility are discussed.

Waldo Beach, *The Christian Life* (Richmond: The CLC Press, 1966), the first adult study book on Christian ethics in the Covenant Life Curriculum.

Isabel Rogers, *In Response to God* (Richmond: The CLC Press, 1969), the second adult study book on Christian ethics in the Covenant Life Curriculum.

Other books I have found helpful are cited in the notes.